THE
CHRISTIAN
VIEW
OF
MAN

BY

WILLARD W. WETZEL

UNITED CHURCH PRESS

BOSTON PHILADELPHIA

OTHER MATERIALS FOR THIS COURSE:

The Decision Maker,
a resource book for adults

"The Children of Israel
Worshiping the Golden Calf"
and "The Last Supper,"
teaching pictures in Audio-Visual Packet I

Hymns for Worship—Adult,
a recording in Audio-Visual Packet I

PHOTOGRAPHS: Sheldon Brody 2; Robert Fulton 38, 40;
Jerome Halberstadt 25, 45, 102 (2); Dick Lebowitz 40, 75, 94, 101, 111;
Peter C. Schlaifer 22, 42, 98;
Kenneth Thompson 56 (*Taken at meeting of the
Klu Klux Klan, Savannah, Ga., 7-20-63*), 67

REPRODUCTIONS: Photo Alinari 49;
Anderson 49; The Bettman Archive 72

Copyright © 1963 by the United Church Press.
Printed in the United States of America.
All rights to this book are reserved.
No part of the text or illustrations
may be reproduced in any form
without written permission of the publishers,
except brief quotations used in connection
with reviews in magazines or newspapers.

The scripture quotations in this publication
are from the *Revised Standard Version of the Bible,*
copyrighted 1946 and 1952 by the
Division of Christian Education,
National Council of Churches,
and used by permission.
This book is part of the
United Church Curriculum,
prepared and published by the
Division of Christian Education and
the Division of Publication
of the United Church Board for Homeland Ministries.

Library of Congress Catalog Card No. 63–19207

CONTENTS

INTRODUCTION

GUIDELINES FOR PLANNING

UNIT I—EXPLORING OUR NATURE

UNIT II—EXPLORING OUR PARADOXICAL NATURE

UNIT III—EXPLORING THE CHRISTIAN HERITAGE

UNIT IV—EXPLORING THE CHALLENGE IN THE CHRISTIAN HERITAGE

APPENDIX

Introduction

We do not often think of it in such terms, but there is no question more important than that of the nature and purpose of our lives. Who am I? What am I like? Why am I here? What does God expect of my life? Such questions are coming back into currency as Christians join all the earth's children in examining the conflicting views of man.

Sociologists tell us that contemporary man is aimless, that his life lacks purpose and direction. His condition, we are told, often is one of little hope and less joy. Yet this is also a day in which the urge—and the wherewithal—to grapple with such fundamental issues holds the promise of helping us to achieve a deeper-than-ever level of understanding of ourselves. If our study of the nature and purpose of our being bears any fruit at all, we may—by the grace of God—still be able to transform the "rat race" into a pilgrimage for and under God.

The Purpose of the Course

This course is designed to lead adult study groups into a meaningful—and, hopefully, a life-changing—exploration of the Christian view of the nature and purpose of man. The purpose of the course is *that adults may grow in their understanding of the realities on which the Christian teachings about man are based; that they may be inwardly strengthened and have their daily relationships transformed by entering ever more fully into a right relationship with God as revealed in Jesus Christ.*

1

The Scope of the Course

In attempting to achieve this purpose, the course provides opportunities for gaining a deeper understanding of the Christian conception of man as contrasted with the current secular conceptions of man.

It seeks to lift up the constant struggle that takes place within man and keeps him from achieving his fullest potentialities and capacities because of the distortion of his relationship with God.

It tries to provide an opportunity for adults to think through the meanings of life and the Christian faith in a systematic manner so that they may arrive at a clearer understanding of God's purpose for their lives.

It hopes to challenge adults to reexamine their own lives in the light of their deepening awareness of the reality of God as revealed in Jesus Christ, and to stimulate them to grow in their willingness to accept God's grace and to respond to his redemptive love.

The Point of View of the Course

There is considerable misunderstanding about human nature—its limitations, its possibilities, and the place that man occupies in the entire realm of creation. Adults experience conflicting tendencies within themselves each day. Sometimes they are too self-satisfied, while at other times they are too discontented. Most adults are seeking a way out of their emotional and intellectual difficulties, and are wondering about their own worth, their security, their destiny.

Although secular views of man include some valid insights with respect to the human situation, they appear incomplete when compared to the understanding of man presented in the Christian, biblical view of man.

The Christian view sees man as the chief work of God, with a high status—little lower than God himself. His lack of complete trust in God, however, causes him to fall prey to sin. His tendency to strive to be what he should not be, or to seek a range of liberty beyond his capacities, contributes to his difficulties and causes frustrations and anxieties.

A person's lack of a sense of vocation, his feeling that his work is unimportant or that what he is doing is socially insignificant, his desire to be economically and socially successful, his eagerness for security and recognition—all cause him to do what he knows he should not: to seek shortcuts to achieve his goals, to become selfishly ambitious, and to nurture jealousy and hatred. Succumbing to the selfward pull of his nature, he inflicts injuries upon himself and involves others in this process; he changes utterly the nature of his life, his relations with others, and his relationship with God.

When man relies upon himself, he is incapable of countering the perverse pull of human nature: "I do not do what I want, but I do the very thing I hate" (Romans 7:15). But when man accepts God as the central factor in his life, he is enabled to transcend some of his frustrations and to reach deeper and more fruitful levels of relationships with both God and his fellowmen.

Responding to God's claim involves, among other things, a continual growth in one's understanding of what man is, what his relationships to God should be, and what acceptance of the demands of the faith means. There is no painless and easy way by which a person can be restored to his God-given place. Only by the intervention of God can a person rise above the consequences of his nonconstructive choices. This intervention has been accomplished for all men through the life, death, and resurrection of Jesus Christ; but the effectiveness of each person's action depends upon his willingness to accept the power of God's forgiving love.

Awareness of God's constant presence in the continuing power of the Holy Spirit, identification with the Christian fellowship, recognition of the power of prayer, and an understanding of how others deal with their frustrations and anxieties—all of these influence a person's relationship with God and with fellowmen. These help a person gain a clearer understanding of himself, his abilities, and his potentialities. In so doing, they point over and over again to the redeeming power of God revealed in Jesus Christ.

The Unifying Theme

A complete course in itself, THE CHRISTIAN VIEW OF MAN is also part of a larger plan: the United Church Curriculum. It is prepared as a course for adults in a semester in which the theme that unifies the work of all age levels is "Exploring Our Christian Heritage."

For many church school classes this will mean that they will be using the course during the five-month semester from February through June of 1964. This is the second semester of the first year of the United Church Curriculum. Other church school classes will be using this course at a later date, as an elective, or at a meeting time other than Sunday mornings. Still other adult groups will be using the course in such experiences as Sunday evening or weeknight sessions, in teachers' study meetings, in weekend retreats, in schools of religion, in Bible study groups, or as program resource material for lay groups.

Whenever and in whatever circumstances you are using this course, you will be devoting yourselves to an exploration of the Christian heritage—especially of the Bible—in an effort to develop a deeper understanding of the Christian view of the nature and purpose of man.

4

Guidelines for Planning

In other areas of life we are accustomed to saying that you get out of something only what you put into it. Planning is not all there is to leading an adult study group, but it is an indispensable part of the process. It is our hope, therefore, that you will give thorough attention to the following guidelines for planning.

If we were to try to issue a guarantee for the success of your course (however you define *success*), one thing we would include in the conditions of the warranty is that the leader must do more than look at the session suggestions for Sunday morning during the previous week. For the guarantee to be effective, it would be essential that the leader of the group go through *all* the coursebook and resource book (*The Decision Maker*) as early as possible. Some of the suggestions made in the session plans are of such a nature that they are not much work if arranged for early, but almost impossible at the last minute. (For instance: the duplication of a form for listing influences that affect our decisions—an important ingredient of unit four.)

This preparatory look at the entire course will also serve to give you some indication of the four-unit organization of the course, of the purpose of the course and of the units, and of the way in which the Bible, the two teaching pictures, the hymns for worship, and the resource book are used in the development of the course.

Later sections of "Guidelines for Planning" will tell you how to plan a schedule for the course so that you will have some overall idea of which session you will be considering on which day. But you will want to be flexible in your use of these tentative plans, allowing for the development of the course according to the interests of your group. Do not feel that you must cover everything. Far better to have gone down deep and come up moved than to have been content merely to skim the surface in an attempt to keep a neat schedule.

Methods, Objectives, and Procedures

The question of what methods to employ in study groups of adults is often a difficult one. This course assumes that your group is sincere about the task of Christian education to the point of being willing to venture into small-group study of the Bible, and perhaps even into the use of posters, evaluation forms, and role-playing. But we have tried to make sure that in each case where such a method is suggested an alternate procedure is also offered.

The method that is basic to the course and is used most frequently is small-group study of the Bible. If your group is not in the habit of doing this, you will find it easy to learn and the results well worth the effort involved. Simply prepare instructions in advance, either on a poster or on a piece of paper for each small group. Then divide into small groups of not less than three and not more than seven persons each.

Sometimes leaders of rather large study groups feel that it is not possible for them to use small-group study of the Bible. In experimenting with this course we subdivided a group of seventy-five adults into small groups of six or seven persons each—all meeting in the same room. The discussion was truly animated. Whenever you have more than twenty to twenty-five persons in an adult study group, however, every effort should be made to subdivide.

The other methods that we are suggesting involve visualizing the subject or having individual members of the group do things for themselves instead of listening passively. These suggestions are made because it is our understanding that persons tend to remember only about ten percent of what they *hear,* fifty or sixty percent of what they *see,* and eighty-five or ninety percent of what they *do!*

You will perhaps observe that the course does not often state precisely where your group should "come out." The course offers no pat answers because there are no pat answers to the questions with which we are involved in this course. We think the important thing is to ask the right questions and discuss them seriously and deeply.

Our guess is that if your study group detects that you are not gunning for pat answers the members of the group will get into the discussion much more readily.

Methods are never to be used as gimmicks or as ends in themselves. Rather, method is always related to an end or purpose. For example, if it is information you want to convey in a short amount of time and in a systematic manner, lecture (or presentation) is an excellent method. But, on the other hand, when attitudes and opinions are to be considered in the light of the Christian heritage, and perhaps altered, then discussion is a far superior method.

The strategy is to determine what is involved in *being* Christian. This will help you to formulate the objective of your sessions, and to decide upon the method or combination of methods that will most effectively and efficiently achieve your objective. In most cases you will want to use methods in combination. For example, in planning for a discussion you will recognize that the group has acquired the necessary information prior to the session (as by reading the resource book and the Bible) or you will need to include in your group session some method of presenting information—such as a lecture, filmstrip, reading or exhibit. When you plan for the presentation of information, you will almost always want to combine this with a listening team, a panel discussion, buzz groups, or role-playing, in order that members of the group may gain insights and develop an understanding of the information.

In your designing of a creative combination of procedures you should follow certain important principles. One of these is that the *members of your group will participate more freely in learning experiences they have helped to plan* than in experiences that you have planned for them. This means that you should take seriously all the suggestions of this course for involving members of your group in evaluation and planning, especially the use of evaluation forms and the appointment of a steering committee. (See the paragraphs about the constructive use of evaluation, page 20.)

Another important principle is that *new knowledge will be accepted, remembered, and utilized more readily if it is provided in response to the recognition of the need for it* than when it is offered merely because the course includes it. This suggests that a person is more interested in answers to questions he has raised than in answers to questions that you think he ought to be asking.

There are two implications of this principle: (1) Teaching involves us in learning to *listen*. Often we tend to prescribe before we have made a diagnosis, which usually takes more time and energy than the prescription. (2) It may be more helpful to arrange our group sessions to allow for questions *before* lectures, filmstrips, and book reviews, as well as afterward.

A third principle of great importance in designing your combinations of teaching methods is that *the more actively we participate the more we learn*. This suggests that in every case where there is a choice among methods of accomplishing an objective, priority should be given to the one that provides the most involvement. This principle also suggests that when you use passive methods such as lectures you can vastly improve their effectiveness by combining them with techniques that necessitate involvement—such as may be gained by listening teams, reaction panels, buzz groups, and group discussions.

Finally, persons remember and respond more readily to *experiences that are sparkling and dynamic* than to those that are dull and routine. This suggests that teachers should strive for freshness of approach, novelty, balance, variety, and vividness, and should be concerned about creating a group climate of warm and trustful relationships.

In general, *we teach as much by relationships as by content*. Often a leader is so anxious to cover every point in his outline that he forgets to be concerned for the persons in the group—for their relationships, their interests, their needs. When this happens "teaching" becomes a superficial and shallow dealing with trivialities and generalities, and the class relationships may be so superficial that persons are unable and unwilling to share with one another their real problems and concerns.

We need to make every effort to establish a climate of compassionate love and to attain a deeper understanding of what is involved in being Christian. Certainly your group will not perfectly create the climate you desire. But isn't the matter of relationships worth putting above the mere transmission of content as the objective of your sessions? Then the transmission of content becomes really significant, and you will find that not only will the content be welcomed with a new eagerness, but it will also be remembered and utilized in daily living.

The chart that follows is not meant to be definitive or exhaustive, but suggestive of the way in which methods are related to objectives and purposes:

OBJECTIVE OR PURPOSE	POSSIBLE METHODS
The Transmission of *information*	Reading and Research, Lectures, Audio-Visuals, Field Trips, Exhibits, Interviews of Resource Persons
The Development of *insights and understanding*	Problem-solving Discussion, Buzz Groups, Assignments for Writing, Listening Teams, Reaction Panels, Role-playing
The Development of *attitudes*	Role-playing, Permissive Discussion, Individual Counseling, Field Trips, Biographical Reading, Visits with Great Personalities
The Acquisition of *skills*	Demonstration, Role-playing, Observation and Evaluation, Practice

An Associate Leader: Your Notebook

It takes time to keep a notebook, and perhaps you are the kind of person who does not enjoy writing things down. But an accurate record of the highlights of your session can be an associate leader. And if you do not enjoy doing it yourself, perhaps this is something with which a member of the group can help you. Just be sure that the notes are brief and concise. A loose-leaf notebook is handiest to use, and it might include such things as the following:

1. The calendar and schedule for the entire course, suggestions for the development of which are contained in the section entitled "A Bird's-eye View of the Course."

2. Pertinent information such as age, occupation, hobbies, education, and experience of each member of the group.

3. Session plans. (Suggestions for the development of session plans and one sample session plan are included in this coursebook.)

4. An evaluation of each class session. The best time to put notes in writing is as soon as possible after the session is concluded.

5. Ideas for future sessions of the group. It is extremely helpful to get these into writing before they slip away.

6. Any newspaper clippings, stories, pictures, cartoons, and the like that might be used as discussion starters in sessions of the group. Perhaps you will want to keep the clippings in a large envelope attached to the inside cover of the notebook.

The Resource Book, *The Decision Maker*

Each person in your study group should have a copy of the resource book entitled *The Decision Maker*. It is organized according to the number of chapters that the subject warrants rather than the number of sessions your group plans to have. Such an organization of the resource book is designed to give the subject the balanced treatment that its content demands.

It is very important for you to explain the nature of the resource book to your group, especially if they have been accustomed to a week-by-week book. Be sure to help them understand that this is a paperback reading book of the kind they would buy in a bookstore. As such it may be studied in its entirety as early in the course as possible.

The chapter headings in the resource book indicate the general subject areas of the course. Chapter one tells of the paradox in our nature. It claims that we are a riddle to ourselves. Chapters two, three, four, and five explore the several aspects of this paradox. The remaining chapters of the book explore the Christian heritage and its challenge.

This Coursebook, THE CHRISTIAN VIEW OF MAN

The book that you are now reading—THE CHRISTIAN VIEW OF MAN—is called the coursebook. It gives suggestions for the organization and administration of the course, how to prepare for sessions, and what procedures might be followed. You will want to give a copy to anyone related to the leadership of the group. Some groups also prefer to give a copy to every person.

The subdivisions of the course are called units. You will notice that the course is divided into four units, four major subdivisions into which this subject logically falls. As is shown by "A Bird's-eye View of the Course" on pages 15–19, the first unit is concerned with the fact that man by nature is paradoxical. Unit II is concerned with exploring first one and then the other aspect of this paradox. Unit III leads us into an exploration of the Christian heritage on the nature and purpose of human existence. Unit IV considers the challenge in the Christian heritage.

Unit numbers are given in roman numerals and session numbers in arabic numerals. For example, I–2 indicates session two of unit one; III–3 means session three of unit three; and IV–2 means session two of unit four. The pages of this coursebook are numbered consecutively from 1 to 128 and by unit and session numbers. The latter numbers are made up of roman and arabic numerals.

The numbering of the sessions is done by unit and session rather than by session alone because this allows greater flexibility in the use of the course, and encourages members of your group to think in terms of its natural subdivisions.

The coursebook material is arranged for seventeen to twenty-one sessions. Some groups will want to use the course in more sessions; others will want to use it in short-term study (such as six- or ten-week courses). On occasion the resource book may be used at a retreat. In the unit introductions we suggest how some of the sessions can be combined if you have less than twenty-one sessions available, but this is by no means the only way to rearrange the course to fit it to your needs and to your schedule. You will want to tailor the course to your particular situation.

It is expected that most of the sessions will contain more material than can profitably be discussed. Do not feel bound to follow every suggestion, but try to make each experience significant.

Worship and *Hymns for Worship—Adult*

This course assumes that the primary purpose of the adult study group is study—set in a framework of devotion. Adults' primary experience of corporate worship is to be found in the church service.

If you are meeting as a Sunday morning church school class, therefore, a closing (or opening) prayer or hymn should be sufficient. If you are meeting at a time other than Sunday morning, you may want to have a slightly more elaborate period of worship.

You will observe that we also recommend that the worship come at the conclusion rather than at the beginning of the session. More and more groups find that worship is more meaningful then. The entire session becomes a preparation for worship, with devotions as the climax. Moreover, you can begin your study session promptly, without waiting until all have arrived.

The recording *Hymns for Worship—Adult* is included in Audio-Visual Packet I and is intended for use with this course. The recording is the reverse side of the record for the filmstrip entitled *Five Parables of Jesus.*

Hymns for Worship—Adult consists of five hymns sung by the senior choir of the First Congregational Church of Wellesley Hills, Massachusetts. Each hymn is introduced by a commentary, sometimes including the reading of a passage of scripture or a prayer. Each hymn and its related material is on a separate band.

The contents include:

BAND 1: Psalm 90; Commentary; "Our God, Our Help in Ages Past" (verses 1, 2, 3, and 6). 4 minutes.

BAND 2: Prayer of General Confession; Commentary; "Lord, Thy Mercy Now Entreating" (verses 1, 2, 4, and 5). 4 minutes.

BAND 3: Commentary; Psalm 46; "A Mighty Fortress Is Our God" (verses 1 and 4). 5 minutes.

BAND 4: Commentary; "All Hail the Power of Jesus' Name" (verses 1, 4, and 5). 3 minutes.

BAND 5: Commentary; "Breathe on Me, Breath of God" (verses 1 and 3). 2½ minutes.

Suggestions for the use of these materials appear in the various sessions. You will undoubtedly find many other uses for this record.

The Two Teaching Pictures

There are two teaching pictures for this course in Audio-Visual Packet I. Both are reproductions of classical paintings.

"The Children of Israel Worshiping the Golden Calf" by Nicholas Poussin is intended for use with unit II of this course. It is related to chapter two of the resource book, on the subject of idolatry—and it should also be used at the conclusion of the course, in review.

"The Last Supper" by Fra Angelico is intended for use with units III and IV. It can be used with the sessions of unit III that are based on chapter seven of the resource book, "The Redeemer." It can be used with the sessions of unit IV in which the Lord's Supper is discussed as the reenactment of God's redemption, and God's call for us to respond to his kind of love.

Additional Resources

We have endeavored to make this a self-contained course. This means that we believe that you can have an interesting and productive study of the Christian view of man by using nothing more than the Bible, this coursebook, and the resource book. We assume that your church will have purchased Audio-Visual Packet I, which will make available the two teaching pictures and the recording *Hymns for Worship—Adult*. If you do not have the packet, both the pictures and the recording can be purchased separately.

Since church libraries are continually increasing their resources, and more individuals are purchasing books, recordings, and pictures for their homes, we do make suggestions as to additional resources. In each case, however, these are optional and not essential to the integrity of the course. In most cases they are listed in separate sections at the conclusion of the session suggestions.

In several of the sessions we suggest the use of a portion of the recording of Handel's *Messiah*. This is so generally available that we assume that most groups will be able to obtain it for their use. If you cannot, however, do not worry about the lack of it. Also, in session 1 of unit II we suggest the use of a recording of a scriptural speech drama entitled *The Speak Four Trio*. This recording has other passages of scripture in addition to the Genesis creation story which we recommend and would have much use in your study groups. It is published by the Word Record Company, and is record

W-4013-P. It is available from H. Royer Smith, 10 Walnut St., Philadelphia, Pa. 19107.

We suggest that you may want to ask the church school or church to purchase this excellent record. However, it too is an optional additional resource not required for the integrity of your learning experience.

For leaders who want additional resource material, the following books are helpful:

ON THE CHRISTIAN VIEW OF MAN—

The Christian Man by William Hamilton, part of the Layman's Theological Library. Westminster Press, Philadelphia, 1956. A very readable book. Especially helpful is its stress on the centrality of forgiveness in the Christian life.

What Is the Nature of Man? The subtitle is "Images of Man in Our American Culture." Christian Education Press, Philadelphia, 1959. This book by sixteen authors is a bit more difficult reading, but has many valuable insights.

The Nature and Destiny of Man by Reinhold Niebuhr. Charles Scribner's Sons, New York, 1941 and 1943. *The* classic in the field, for those who want to really dig into the subject. In two volumes.

The Heidelberg Catechism, 400th Anniversary Edition, 1563–1963. Translated from the original German and Latin texts by Allen O. Miller and M. Eugene Osterhaven. Copyright 1962 by United Church Press.

ON IDOLATRY AND PSEUDO-RELIGIONS—

Modern Rivals to the Christian Faith by Cornelius Loew, a part of the Laymen's Theological Library. The Westminster Press, Philadelphia, 1956. Inexpensive to buy, and excellent resource material.

ON LOVE AS CENTRAL IN THE CHRISTIAN RELIGION—

Herein Is Love, by Reuel L. Howe. Judson Press, Valley Forge, 1961.
On the Love of God by John McIntyre. Harper & Row, New York, 1962. Discusses how love is concern, commitment, communication, community, involvement, identification, response, and responsibility.

14

Understanding Ourselves As Adults by Paul B. Maves. Published for the Cooperative Publishing Association by Abingdon Press, New York and Nashville, 1959. A Leadership Training Text. Contains excellent chapters on such things as the nature and interests of adults, their developmental tasks, their motivations, and their manner of operation.

Learning Together in the Christian Fellowship by Sara Little. John Knox Press, Richmond, Virginia, 1956. An inexpensive book of relatively few pages, though exceedingly helpful.

Creative Methods for Adult Classes by John McKinley. Bethany Press, St. Louis, 1960. Same comments apply as for the above listed book.

Adult Education Procedures, A Handbook of Tested Patterns for Effective Participation, by Paul Bergevin, Dwight Morris, Robert M. Smith. The Seabury Press, Greenwich, Conn., 1963. The most complete handbook available. It gives helpful diagrams and post-session checklists. It also gives help on planning.

On Organization and Administration of Adult Study Groups—

A Manual for Adults by Walter E. Dobler. United Church Press, 1963. The age-group manual at the adult level of the United Church Curriculum.

About the Sample Session Plan

Be sure to *write* some form of session plan, however simple it may be. In order to show you how one of the session plans of this course might look in written form, we have included a sample session plan, written out in full: session 1 of unit I. Certainly you will want to adapt this to your own needs, or "start from scratch" in the development of your own. Remember, this is only a sample.

A Bird's-eye View of the Course

Your notebook should contain a chart or listing of the sessions and dates on which your group plans to meet. This is especially important in light of the fact that the course is developed in units, with several sessions under each unit. On pages 17–19 you will find sample outlines of the units and sessions.

The course is divided into units because five months is an overly long period of time for a sustained study on one subject. The unit division allows a greater sense of accomplishment and completion, and gives opportunity for more frequent evaluation and possible redirection of the course.

To get a picture of the blocks of time you will have available for the course, list the dates of all meetings of your group. Alongside the appropriate dates, write any fixed events that will prevent the meeting of your group. Try to foresee as many as possible of the times when your session will be either shortened or canceled.

This timetable will help you think about your plans for the semester. Try to arrange the units (and sessions in them) to fit the timetable as seems best for your group.

A sample of such a timetable and schedule appears on the following pages. You will want to have something similar to it in your notebook. If you want to give the members of your group an idea of the agenda of the course, there are several ways of doing it. You might mimeograph the listing of the schedule and tentative session titles. Or you might letter it on newsprint paper or chalkboard, or simply read it aloud to the group.

Our suggestion is that, however you present the tentative schedule to your study group, you begin by giving them only the titles of the four units and the detailed outline of the first unit. If you give them the entire outline at the beginning, it will take away much of the flexibility that you might otherwise achieve. Also, be sure to stress the fact that the outline is tentative and that you expect to revise it according to the interests of the group as you proceed with the actual sessions of the course.

The following is one way in which you might outline the units and the tentative schedule for the first unit. You will want to adapt this sample to the needs of your own group, or even develop an entirely different one. Sample charts include spaces for tentative session dates.

COURSE PURPOSE: That adults may grow in their understanding of the realities on which the Christian teachings about man are based; that they may be inwardly strengthened and have their daily experiences transformed by entering ever more fully into a right relationship with God as revealed in Jesus Christ.

Unit I—Exploring Our Nature

A two- or three-session introductory unit that raises the question of the basic nature of man. Is man basically good, or bad—or both? We learn that he is a puzzling combination of both.

Unit II—Exploring Our Paradoxical Nature

A five- or six-session unit that delves into the various aspects of the riddle that we are. We learn that we are creatures of incredible potential, limited only by our constant dependency upon God; but that we tend to rebel against this dependency.

Unit III—Exploring the Christian Heritage

A six- or seven-session unit that explores the Christian heritage on the subject of man's nature and purpose in life, especially as this heritage is recorded in the Bible.

Unit IV—Exploring the Challenge

A four- or five-session unit that delves into the life-changing decision about our response to the kind of love with which God loves us, and that explores the role of our day-by-day decisions in designing a style of life in which we live maturely in freedom—in captivity to the Spirit.

tentative schedule for unit one

SESS.	DATE	TITLE	I–2 RB	BIBLE
I–1		Is Man Basically Good, or Bad?	Ch. 1	Romans 7:13–20 Psalm 8
I–2		The Paradox in our Nature	Ch. 1, 2	Romans 7:15–25 Psalm 8 Psalm 144
I–3		Can Science and Education Solve the Riddle?	Ch. 2, 3	Psalm 8

Later in the course you will want to distribute—in one of the forms we discussed previously—the tentative outline and schedule of the other three units. The following is our sample. You will want to adapt it to your situation or develop an entirely new one.

sample
outline
and
schedule
for
unit
two

SESS.	DATE	TITLE	I–2 RB	BIBLE
II–1		Idolatry Is Rampant	Ch. 2, 3	Exodus 32:1–6 Matthew 6:24, 33 Daniel 3:1
II–2		Significant but Incomplete	Ch. 2, 3	Exodus 32:1–6
II–3		Sins and Sin	Ch. 4	Romans 1:18–23 Genesis 3:1–7
II–4		Am I Really a Sinner?	Ch. 4	Genesis 3:1–7 Romans 3:23 Matthew 19:16–17 Jeremiah 17:5–8
II–5		The Image of God	Ch. 5	Genesis 1:26–31 Colossians 1:15–20
II–6		Potential Incredible	Ch. 5	Genesis 1:26–31 Genesis 2:4b–9 Psalm 8

sample
outline
and
schedule
for
unit
three

SESS.	DATE	TITLE	I–2 RB	BIBLE
III–1		The Need for Recurring Rescue	Ch. 6	2 Cor. 5:16–21 Luke 18:9–14 Romans 8:3–4
III–2		Christ: The Difference Between the Covenants	Ch. 7	Deut. 6:4–6 Lev. 19:18 Matt. 5:17 Rom. 13:10 Heb. 9:11–22 2 Cor. 3:6

SESS.	DATE	TITLE	I-2 RB	BIBLE
III–3		The Old Covenant and the Law	Ch. 6	Gal. 3:19–29 Rom. 7:7–12 Ex. 20:1–20 Deut. 5 Ex. 34:10–26 Matt. 5:17
III–4		Love that Fulfills the Law	Ch. 7, 8	Matt. 5:43–48 Matt. 20:1–16
III–5		Redemption in Love	Ch. 7, 8	Matt. 20:1–16 John 13:31–35 1 John 4:19 Matt. 5:43–48
III–6		Justice in Love	Ch. 7, 8	Matt. 25:31–46 Matt. 5:17–20 John 14:15–24
III–7		Tension in Love	Ch. 9	Same as previous three sessions plus Psalm 51

SESS.	DATE	TITLE	I-2 RB	BIBLE
IV–1		Can I Love as Christ Does?	Ch. 9	John 13:34–35 Matt. 5:43–48 Matt. 19:17
IV–2		Growing in Grace: The Process of Gratitude	Ch. 9	Eph. 2:1–10 Matt. 18:23–35
IV–3		Freedom in Captivity	Ch. 10	Rom. 6:15–23 Gal. 5:13–26
IV–4		Responsible Decision Making	Ch. 10	Joshua 24:14–15 Acts 21:13–14
IV–5		The Spirit in Our Decisions	Ch. 10	Acts 2:1–21

sample
outline
and
schedule
for
unit
four

The Constructive Use of Evaluation

Evaluation is a great asset in planning. We have tried to build evaluation into the fabric of the course, and hope that you will make constructive use of it, even if it is a new departure. If you have not done it before, only the sincere use of the process will give you some idea of its great value. Your planning ahead will be much more effective if it is preceded by a backward look.

An opinion blank is suggested for session 1 of unit I. We think that an examination of the blank on page 32 will be sufficient to convince you that it is well worth the time and effort needed to duplicate copies and use them at the conclusion of the session.

Other forms are printed in this coursebook on pages 39 and 70. Many other forms are available from other sources. One of the best sources is *Christians Learning for Christian Living*, the introductory course in the adult curriculum of the Disciples of Christ. It is part of the Christian Discipleship Series, published by the Christian Board of Publication, St. Louis.

Leaders of adult groups have found steering committees of great assistance in evaluating past sessions and in planning for future sessions. Such a committee usually consists of three or more members of the group who volunteer, or who are selected by the leader of the group to serve for a stated period of time, such as five months, during which a whole course can be covered.

We suggest that such a committee meet five times during the course of the five-month semester. It should meet as soon as possible after the following sessions: session 1 of unit I; session 3 of unit I (the completion of unit I); the final session of unit II; the final session of unit III; and at the conclusion of the course, at which time you should raise questions about following up the course.

This committee will be able to utilize the opinion blanks and to evaluate them with you, as well as to supplement them with personal opinions and observations.

Short-Term Use of the Resource Book

If you have occasion to use the resource book in short-term study of the Christian view of man, you may well be interested in the following outline of scripture passages and questions which was submitted to members of a group for use in preparing for participating in five sessions of one-and-a-half to two hours each.

I. Romans 7:13–20
  1. Are we more apt to be good than bad, or bad than good?
  2. Does education make us "good"?
II. Genesis 1:26–31; Romans 3:9–12; 21–26
  1. What does *image* mean?
  2. What is sin? Am I really a sinner?
III. Deuteronomy 5:1–5; Job 19:23–29
  1. What is the difference between the old covenant and the new covenant?
  2. Which counts more in the Christian life: what I know or who I know? Why?
IV. Matthew 20:1–16; Matthew 25:31–46
  1. What is the one main point of the parable in Matthew 20?
  2. What is meant by Christian love?
  3. What is meant by redemptive love?
  4. What is forgiveness? What is the relationship between love and justice?
V. Romans 6; Joshua 24:14, 15
  1. Are you saved?
  2. What is more important in the Christian life, goodness or thankfulness?
  3. What is freedom?
  4. What is maturity?
  5. What is the one main purpose of your life?
  6. What is success?

Session plan suggestions in the coursebook may help you to develop plans from this outline. For example, session 1 was based on unit I of the coursebook, while session 2 was based on unit II. Session 3 was based on sessions 1, 2, 3, and 4 of unit III of the coursebook. Session 4 was based on sessions 5, 6, and 7 of unit III of the coursebook, while the final session (5) was based on unit IV of the coursebook.

Thoughts for the Leader

A quotation appears at the beginning of each session of this coursebook. At various places the session suggestions refer to these as the "Thought for the Leader." These quotations are meant for the leader to meditate upon and for him to use as resource material for sessions of the study group whenever they seem useful.

Unit I
EXPLORING
OUR NATURE

Consisting of but two or three sessions, Unit I is a short section of the course. It serves to introduce the course and to establish the fact that we are riddles to ourselves. On the one hand we have an essential goodness and extremely high status as the highest of God's creatures. Our potential is virtually unlimited. On the other hand, we have the tendency to forfeit this high status by striving to be equal to and like God. This is the essence of the deepest revelation of sin by the Bible.

Science and education—as well as other aspects of life—give power, ability, and motivation to our efforts at improvement and service, as long as they are under God. But when men succumb to the temptation to elevate them to the inordinate status of pseudo-religions or idols, their incompleteness becomes manifest. They are relevant but incomplete explanations of the puzzle of man's nature.

The first session of this unit raises the question: Is man basically good, or bad? It includes a fully written sample session plan, showing how one group went about the beginning of the course. The idea of this session, in addition to introducing the course, is to study Romans 7:13–20, in which Paul speaks of the riddle that he is—finding both good and bad in his nature.

Session 2 makes the affirmation that our nature is a paradox. It continues the thoughts unfolded in session 1, and gives opportunity for deepening our realization of the startling truth that our nature is puzzling. It is based on Romans 7:21–25.

Optional session 3 asks whether or not science and education can solve the riddle that we are. It makes use of portions of chapter three of the resource book.

Is Man Basically Good, or Bad?

*No discussion of the Christian understanding
of man can be right if it so glories in the goodness
of creation as to obscure the reality of "the fall," or so
grovels in the depravity of "the fall" as to
deny the goodness of creation. . . .
From the point of view of creation, man is good.
God cannot make a bad world or a bad man. . . .
Nevertheless, looked at the opposite way,
at his* actual *nature, . . . man is undeniably bad. . . .
God made man good. This is his essential nature.
Man's fallen nature is not his real nature, but only the
actual condition of his nature. He is in alien territory
but he is still a citizen of heaven.*[1]

Purpose of This Session

To become familiar with the nature and purpose of the course; to whet our appetites by dipping into the first unit; to raise the question: Is man basically good—or bad?

Background for the Leader

It is our opinion that in the first session of a course you should be careful to take sufficient time for the introduction of the course as a whole and for involving all members of the group in planning for the direction you will take. As you can see by the sample lesson plan, we believe that this involves taking the time to talk about the nature and purpose of the course and to examine the resources for the course (resource book, teaching pictures, *Hymns for Worship—Adult,* Bible, and your notebook).

You should also devise some method of giving members of your group the opportunity and the responsibility of expressing their opinion as to what should go into this course. At the conclusion of the session, use the opinion blank included with the sample session plan. (See page 32.)

In your study of Romans 7 you will want to focus on the question: Is man basically good, or bad? The result of this session should be the realization that man is both good and bad. We are riddles to ourselves. The "Thought for the Leader" states the case exceptionally well. You will probably want to share it with the group.

Getting Started

This would be the time for the display of all of the resources available for the task in which this course engages you. You will probably want to have the purpose of the course prominently displayed, and you may want to label your resources as your "tools." The resources to display would include this coursebook; the resource book entitled *The Decision Maker;* the two teaching pictures, "The Children of Israel Worshiping the Golden Calf" and "The Last Supper"; and the recording of worship resources, *Hymns for Worship—Adult.* Also include the Bible in your display, for in a real sense it is your resource book. Those who arrive early might be encouraged to examine these resources for the course.

As another aspect of your display you might gather as many pictures of people and groups of people as you can from magazines and other sources. Perhaps you have access to a statue of a man, or a painting. Perhaps you will want to make a poster bearing the question: What is the nature and purpose of man? This would be a dramatic way of visualizing the course.

In our sample session plan we assume that you will want to begin your study with the arrival of the first person. We have provided for this by suggesting that as persons arrive you direct them—after they have seen the resource materials—into small study groups. When they get to their places, they will find written or typed instructions to study Romans 7:13–20, and to ask themselves what this biblical passage says about the basic nature of men.

Getting into Things

If you go directly into small study groups as soon as persons arrive, you will not have your greeting and your introduction of the course and of the resources until after the small-group study. The sample session plan is organized on this assumption in order to make it possible to begin the session when persons begin arriving. An alternative would be to give people more of an opportunity to examine the resources as they arrive, and then start your session at the given hour with a greeting and the introduction of the course.

However you choose to organize your session, the two things that you really want to get into in this session are the introduction of the course (including the purpose of the course and the titles and purposes of the various units) and the study of Romans 7:13–20. The question to consider in the study of this passage from Romans 7 is whether man is basically good, or bad—or both. This study will help you to realize that Paul had the same inner struggle that we all experience. We are a puzzling mixture of doing the good we desire to do and succumbing to the lesser things in life that we really wish to avoid. It will be very helpful to your group if you can help them realize that such tensions are characteristic of everyone, and are certainly not indications of abnormality.

Concluding the Session

It is very important to save the final five or ten minutes of this first session for the use of an opinion blank like the sample on page 32 of this book. This will give you valuable guidance in designing forthcoming sessions so as to help people find answers to the questions they are really asking instead of supplying them with information for which they have no sense of need.

Take It Easy

As you can see, we have suggested an ambitious amount of material for this first session—more than many groups will use—but our experience with the preparation of resource materials indicates that some groups will need this much material. If you cannot cover this much material, plan for a session in which you feel comfortable. Always take it easy. Depth and comprehension are always more important than hastily "covering"—at a superficial level—all that is suggested for you. Here is where you must tailor the resources to your own situation.

Possibilities for Worship

Romans 7:13–20; Psalm 8
Hymn: "Make Me a Captive, Lord"

Is Man Good or Bad?

A SAMPLE PLAN FOR THE FIRST SESSION OF UNIT I

(The plan and the tentative time suggestions which follow are based on an actual session. They are, however, only a sample of how one group proceeded with the first session of the course. You will want to adapt them to your own needs and interests. To use this sample lesson plan as a substitute for doing your own is to invite disaster. Even the course, unit, and session purposes should be "digested" and presented in your own words.)

COURSE PURPOSE (which should be kept in front of the group throughout the entire course, perhaps by posters): That adults may grow in their understanding of the realities on which the Christian teachings about man are based; that they may be inwardly strengthened and have their daily relationships transformed by entering ever more fully into a right relationship with God as revealed in Jesus Christ.

UNIT PURPOSE: To explore man's basic nature, including the significant but incomplete answers to the riddle of his existence that are advanced from secular life.

SESSION PURPOSE: To become familiar with the nature and purpose of this semester's work; to whet our appetites by dipping into the first unit.

PROCEDURE AND TIME SEQUENCE:

A. *Getting Started*—assigning to groups and small-group Bible study .... 15 min.

B. *Introductory Group Session*—leader's presentation (lecture), distribution of suggestions for time schedule (dates for group meetings), purpose, and resource book, together with questions and comments by members of the group .... 15 min.

C. *Getting into the Subject*—leader's comments, with as many reports from small Bible study groups as time will allow .... 15 min.

D. *Concluding and Summarizing*—brief statement of summary, plus assignment for next session .... 5 min.

E. *Evaluation*—time to fill out opinion blanks .... 5 min.

F. *Worship* .... 5 min.

_____

60 min.

Outline of Session Plan

	RESOURCES	MATERIALS
A. Getting Started:		
1. Display pictures of people, as well as objects and artifacts. Display coursebook, resource book, teaching pictures, and recording of *Hymns for Worship—Adult*	Pictures collected from magazines and statues or "models" of people.	Pictures and objects for display.
2. If your group is large or has many new members, you may want to wear a name tag and have each person make and wear a name tag.	List of the members of your group. If this is not available, have paper and pencil on table for signatures.	3″ x 5″ cards, black crayons, pins.
3. Small study groups of not less than three and not more than six persons each. (This can even be done with large groups.)	One paper of instructions for each group. On each paper write or have typed: "Study Romans 7:13–20. What does this say about the basic nature of man? On the basis of past experience and understanding, do you think men are more apt to be bad, or good? Explain."	One paper of instructions for each group.
4. For any group that finishes early, be ready with copies of the resource book, *The Decision Maker.* Ask them to use chapter 1 as an additional resource about man's nature.	Chapter 1 of the resource book, *The Decision Maker.*	One copy of the resource book, *The Decision Maker,* for each person in the group.
B. Introductory Group Session:		
5. Greeting—Welcome	(See notes about this on page 26 of this coursebook.)	Same as under number 4—one copy of the resource book, *The Decision Maker,* for each person in your group.

	RESOURCES	MATERIALS
6. Leader's Presentation about the course **a.** Give title of coursebook and of the resource book. If copies of the resource book have not been distributed, do so now. **b.** Give purpose of the course. **c.** Distribute copies of dates for the group to meet, purpose of the course, and suggested topics.	(See purpose of the course on page 28 of this coursebook.) (See notes about this on page 16 of this coursebook.)	A poster, perhaps a sheet of newsprint, on which has been lettered the purpose of the course. Mimeographed copies of papers on which appear the dates on which the study group will probably meet, and the suggested topics tentatively listed for the dates. (See page 17 of this coursebook).
7. Invite comment or question on the purpose of this semester's work.		
8. Leader make brief presentation about procedure— explain that method is determined largely by purpose. Illustrate by saying: For example, if our purpose is to develop *knowledge*, lecture is still a good method, as well as purposeful reading, audio-visual aids, exhibits, and Bible research. If, on the other hand, our purpose is to develop *understanding*, then problem-solving discussion, case studies, and role-playing are helpful. Our basic method will probably be a combination of presentations and discussions.	Information about methods and their relationship to the purpose the group is striving to achieve. (See page 6 of this coursebook.)	Notes on how to say this well and in a brief period of time. It must be adequately prepared if it is not to take too much time.

9. Mention *resources* that will help us: **a.** Bibles **b.** Resource Book and Coursebook **c.** Leader—who keeps conversation going and on the right track, but does not dominate it. It is somewhat like the role of the prompter in a play. **d.** Group Members—who should get to know all the people in the group and should share their thinking, who will attend regularly, who will read the resource book, and who will occasionally give reactions by filling out opinion blanks. **e.** All persons will share in planning— through opinion blanks and through contributions to members of the steering committee. If chosen, announce. If not chosen, tell how and when members of this committee will be chosen. Explain how the committee will operate.	
C. Getting into the Subject:	
10. Mention unit I and its purpose. Explain that time may not permit reports from all small Bible study groups and that these reports, enriched by a week's thought, will be received next session. If time permits, hear a report or two, but do not take sides about the basic nature of man.	
D. Concluding and Summarizing:	
11. Mention that not only is a consideration of the basic nature and purpose of man vitally important, but also more puzzling than meets the eye. Ask each person to live with Romans 7:13–20 between now and the next session and to read the resource book. Next session we will assume an understanding of at least chapter 1 of the resource book, *The Decision Maker*.	A copy of the Bible and the resource book, *The Decision Maker*, in order to be able to point to Romans 7:13–20 and to the table of contents of the resource book.
E. Evaluating:	
12. Opinion blanks (see sample of one of these on next page). Allow time for filling out. Collect.	
13. A written review made outside the session by the leader, however brief.	
14. If steering committee is functioning, meet with them or ask them to call or write you a brief note on this first session.	

Possibilities for Worship

Romans 7:13–20; Psalm 8

Hymn: "Make Me a Captive, Lord" (suggested course theme hymn.)

SAMPLE OPINION BLANK—FIRST SESSION

1. I think I understand the purpose of this semester's work on the Christian view of man (check one):

   ____ not at all clearly

   ____ some parts not too clearly

   ____ fairly clearly

   ____ very clearly

2. If it were up to me, I would change the purpose of the course in this way (write any changes for improvement): _____

   _____

3. This is a subject (check one):

   ____ of no interest to me

   ____ of some interest to me

   ____ of considerable interest to me

   ____ of intense interest to me

4. Some things I would like to discuss during this course are: _____

   _____

5. I intend to read the resource book, *The Decision Maker,* (check one):

   ____ not at all

   ____ a little bit

   ____ fairly completely

   ____ completely

6. Any other comments or questions: _____

   _____

   _____

The Paradox in Our Nature

God has given man a unique capacity
to know and to respond to him. He created him
in his own image for eternal life. God offered man
the knowledge of good and evil. But such knowledge
can be received only by the taking. It comes through the
making of choices and the discovering of consequences.
By the freedom to make real choices
involving good and evil, God let man become real. He did not
want puppets. God, being no paternalist, created a world
of real risk. On the other hand, in order that
man might not be self-sufficient,
he left him hollow at the center.

Man, therefore, risks falling either in or out,
so to speak, in an attempt either to become secure
by filling in his own emptiness or to find safety by
leaning on others. Not only is man made precarious
within his own nature; he finds precariousness
in nature. Hence his insecurity and anxiety.

Consequently, man works to make himself safe.
He tries to remake himself by self-improvement. He struggles
to conform to what others believe or want. He labors to
lay aside means of security, whether in terms of
working competence or in terms of cash savings. He invests
in friendships, in "connections." [1]

Purpose of This Session

To complete our preliminary look at man's basic nature; to raise the question of his tendency to live as though secular answers were entirely and ultimately adequate.

Getting Started

As persons begin to arrive, ask them to study Romans 7:21–25, either in small groups of six or seven each, or individually. By poster, or verbally, or by instructions written on paper, ask them to think about what Paul is saying in these words. Why does he say, "Wretched man that I am"? Does this make any sense, coming after his dramatic conversion experience? What does it say about the basic nature of man? Is man, by nature, basically good—or bad?

Getting into Things

These are the questions to raise as you lead the group into a discussion of the basic nature of man. You will want to raise the questions and then call for reports from last week's study of Romans 7: 13–20 and from this week's study of Romans 7:21–25.

Keep in mind, and remind the group if necessary, that in this session you are continuing last session's questioning of whether man is good, or bad. You are not trying to delve deeply into either of the two sides of man's nature at this time. You will do that in unit II.

Our feeling is voiced superbly by Nels F. S. Ferré in the "Thought for the Leader" at the head of this session and session 1. You may want to use these statements in the course of your discussion.

Man's nature is *both* good and bad. (See chapter 1 of the resource book, and notice that we stress both.) His nature is paradoxical, or two-sided. On the one hand he is basically good, with a status only slightly lower than that of God himself, and capable of great worth and beauty. On the other hand, despite his high status and potential, he often uses his freedom to do lesser things because of his tendency to shun God. Man is essentially very good and capable of a high destiny, but his tendency is to do the wrong, even when he wants to do better. This is the situation that Paul deplores. Even when we *know* better, and want to *do* better, we find ourselves unable to do so. This is our dilemma—by nature we are both good and bad, and dependent upon a power outside of and greater than ourselves.

What is the opinion of members of your group? How does the feeling in your group compare with the one expressed in the preceding paragraph?

If you have additional time you may find it fruitful to have the group compare Psalm 8:4–8 and Psalm 144:3–8. What view of the nature of man is painted in Psalm 8:4–8? In Psalm 144:3–8? Is it high or low? How high, or how low?

Concluding and Summarizing

Allow a few minutes for summarizing the feelings of the group, and emphasize the fact of the puzzling, paradoxical nature of man. Suggest that future sessions will dig into one and then the other aspect of our nature. At the present time it is important to note only how puzzling and paradoxical we are.

Suggest that the next session will explore the question of whether or not science and education can solve this riddle. It will be based on chapter 3 of the resource book *The Decision Maker* so that this chapter should be studied prior to the next session. It would also be helpful to review chapter 2 of *The Decision Maker*, keeping in mind to question whether or not science and education can solve the riddle we have discussed.

Possibilities for Worship

Prayer
Romans 7:15–25
Hymn: "O for a Closer Walk with God"

Can Science and Education Solve the Riddle?

In the seventeenth century, Pascal wrote: "Christianity is strange. It bids man recognize that he is vile, even abominable; and bids him desire to be like God. Without such a counterpoise, this dignity would make him horribly vain, or this humiliation would make him terribly abject."

Pascal was a highly educated man, one of the greatest physicists and writers of his day; yet in the twentieth century most educated people would reject his saying on both counts. In the first place, they do not like the notion that man is vile. And in the second place, they cannot take seriously the idea that man should desire to be like God.

So from the perspective of many educated people today, Christianity looks not only strange, but also contradictory. And we can easily imagine an enlightened professor saying to Pascal: "Make up your mind. Either wallow in your morbid teaching about man's wickedness, or dream your mystical dreams about his eternal spirit. But by all that is sane and sensible, don't try to have it both ways at once." [1]

Purpose of This Session

To complete unit I by recognizing that man's paradoxical nature is the problem with which he is constantly confronted. The question is what this implies for human life.

Getting Started

This session, based on chapter 3 of the resource book *The Decision Maker*, is exceedingly difficult to plan. The difficulty is in trying to show the vast contributions of such things as science and education when these disciplines serve God, while at the same time noting the temptation to elevate them to the place of God himself by making religions of them. We are really dealing with the problem of idolatry.

The title of chapter 3 of the resource book, "Significant But Incomplete," is an attempt to state the case. The difficulty is that the moment you suggest that science and education cannot offer a *total* explanation of man's needs in life, your hearers assume that you deem science and education insignificant. On the other hand, when you stress their significance, the danger is to deify them.

We suggest that you prepare for this session by asking a teacher and a scientist (or a science teacher) to serve on a panel or in a symposium. Ask the teacher to prepare to speak to the group (for 7 to 10 minutes, depending upon the time you have available) on the importance of education in man's life and the relationship of education to God. Ask the teacher whether he will be willing to participate in a general discussion following the presentations, and whether he will be prepared to comment on the section of chapter 3 which speaks about education *versus* educationism.

Ask the scientist or science teacher to speak on the importance of science in the life of man and on the relationship of science to God. Ask him whether he will be willing to participate in a group discussion, and be prepared to comment on the section of chapter 3 entitled "Scientism."

Be sure to contact these persons as early as possible, and make sure they have copies of the resource book, *The Decision Maker*.

An alternate plan would be to ask members of your own group to assume the roles described above. For example, ask one person to serve as the teacher and another to function as the scientist. There is much to be said for this approach.

Still another possibility would be to have one person read the section in chapter 3 of the resource book entitled "Scientism," while another person would read the section called "Educationism." If time permits, you might also ask a person to read the section, "Patriotism." These persons might be seated as a panel, with you (or someone else in the group) serving as moderator. Small signs in front of the persons would read: Teacher; Scientist; Patriot.

Getting Into Things

These presentations should serve as discussion starters. Following each presentation, or at the end of the total presentation, let the group discuss the issues raised. For example, can education be a pseudo-religion? What does this mean? Can science be an idol? What does this mean? What is a pseudo-religion? An idol?

Concluding and Summarizing

Prepare to have a brief summary of the feeling of the group. If you are moderator of the discussion, you will want to do it. If not you will decide whether to ask the moderator to do it, or to do it yourself at the conclusion of the discussion.

Conclude this unit by mentioning that these sessions mark our introduction to the course. Introduce unit II by giving its theme and its purpose. Mention that the next session will assume prior study of chapter 3 of the resource book *The Decision Maker*.

Possibilities for Worship

Psalm 8

Hymn: "God of Grace and God of Glory"

Prayer, of gratitude for the immensely important contributions of such disciplines as science and education, and a petition for the Spirit of God to keep them in his service

END-OF-SESSION REACTION BLANK

The reaction form below is of a general nature and can be used at the conclusion of any session for which you desire feedback. You will not want to use it at the end of every session, because to do so would invite disinterest and aggravation. On the other hand, you will find it useful at the conclusion of several key sessions of the course. We suggest that you use it after the last session of unit I and at any other time during the course when you feel it will be helpful.

1. In terms of being helpful to me, I would rate this session:
   ____A. Extremely helpful
   ____B. Quite helpful
   ____C. Fairly helpful
   ____D. A little helpful
   ____E. Not at all helpful

2. This session has left unresolved the following questions: _____

_____

3. If I were planning for the next session, I would include:

_____

4. In the near future, but beyond the next session, we should

   consider: _____

_____

5. Other comments: _____

_____

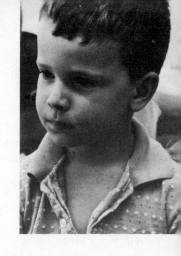

Unit II
EXPLORING OUR PARADOXICAL NATURE

Unit II follows unit I with a five- or six-session study that delves into the various aspects of the riddle that is man. In unit II we learn that we are creatures of incredible potential, limited only by our constant dependence upon God; but that we tend to rebel against dependence upon God and try to make ourselves absolutely free. This is sin—and sin defaces our potential.

If you need to combine two sessions in unit II, we would suggest that you combine II–3 and II–4.

The first session of unit II explores the biblical concern for idolatry and asserts that idolatry is rampant today. It is a study of chapter 2 of the resource book, of Exodus 32, and makes use of the teaching picture "The Children of Israel Worshiping the Golden Calf." In Audio-Visual Packet I–1 of the United Church Curriculum, this picture is a reproduction of a classical painting.

Session II–2 continues the study of idolatry, but with a considerably altered focus. "Significant but Incomplete" is a session in which we take note of the fact that we tend to make idols of some of the most significant aspects of life, and that while these areas of life are genuinely significant, they are incomplete as bases of religious faith.

Session II–3 turns to a different way of examining the same side of the paradox of our human nature. It focuses upon the consideration of the biblical word *sin*. This session stresses the fact that the deepest understanding of sin in the Bible is that it is our declaration of independence from God. Sin is succumbing to our tendency to rebel against God by wanting our freedom to be absolutely unlimited.

The fourth session takes note of the biblical contention that when sin is understood in the terms described in session II–3, sin is universal. Sinners are not special persons or groups. All are sinners. "None is righteous, no not one" (Romans 3:10).

"The Image of God," session II–5, turns to the other side of the paradox that we are. Based on chapter 5 of the resource book, *The Decision Maker,* it examines several of the important implications of being created "in the image of God."

Session II–6 continues the emphasis begun in II–5 by calling attention to our incredible potential when we accept our dependence upon God. It is based on chapter 5 of the resource book and on the study of Psalm 8 and Genesis 1:26–31.

Idolatry is Rampant

*"King Nebuchadnezzar made an image of gold,
whose height was sixty cubits and its breadth six cubits.
He set it up on the plain of Dura, in the province of
Babylon" (Daniel 3:1). This verse has a more contemporary
ring than it could have had in the years before
Hitler's rise. The tyrant ever seeks to make all men bow down
before something he has made. It may be a golden image,
or a racial theory, or a dream of national grandeur,
or military might. They are all alike in that they are
created by men and that they seek to usurp the place of God.
The egocentric man has his idols before which he insists
that others must bow down. They must recognize his gifts,
or his power, or his position of special privilege.
The days of idolatry are never over, and the
madness of putting the idol in God's place is ever with us.
All we do is to refine the idol, but the bowing down
before it is the same crude thing which the king
commanded the Jewish exiles to do.*[1]

Purpose of This Session

To delve more deeply into one side of the paradox of our nature. This session, based on chapter 2 of *The Decision Maker*, deals with the fact that we tend to make things into idols and to build pseudo-religions around them. It recognizes that idolatry is not confined to the past, but is rampant in our lives today.

Background for the Leader

This session and the next one deal with chapters 2 and 3 of the resource book, *The Decision Maker*. This will be a difficult undertaking, not so much because the ideas are complex as because idolatry is the kind of uncomfortable subject that we try to avoid. Of course, we do not try to avoid it consciously; we are usually unaware, when we claim idolatry is no problem in *our* lives, that we are avoiding the facts of the situation.

The important thing in this session, therefore, will be to insist that our search be concerned not so much with our opinions on the matter as with what the Bible says on the subject—and what these biblical experiences mean when they are translated into contemporary terms.

The best way to prepare for this session is to study the "Thought for the Leader" at the head of this and the next session, to study chapter 2 of *The Decision Maker*, and to live with some of the Bible passages mentioned in that chapter: Exodus 32; Judges 2:17; Isaiah 45:20–21; Jeremiah 10:1–10; Matthew 6:24, 33; 1 Corinthians 8:4–6; Galatians 5:19–20; and Acts 7:35–43. The "Thought for the Leader" for this session also cites Daniel 3:1. We suggest that in the session you may want to confine your Bible study to Exodus 32:1–6; Daniel 3:1; and Matthew 6:24, 33.

Getting Started

The secret of success in this session will be to find some way of making idolatry "live." By this we mean that you will need to plan some activity that will help the members of your group realize that this subject is not confined to history books, but is a daily temptation.

We have tried to give impetus to this process by the manner in which chapter 2 of *The Decision Maker* is illustrated. One way to get started would be to have persons examine these illustrations and meditate on them as they arrive.

Since they probably will have seen and reacted to these illustrations before the session, we would suggest several other ways to get started. One would be to prepare a worship center just as you would for any session—except that this time you would substitute some unusual objects for the cross and the Bible. You might make a collection of a miniature house, a scale model of a luxury automobile, a carton of cigarettes, a bottle of perfume, a small American flag, a textbook, and a symbol of science such as a microscope. We would suggest that you make this a collection rather than a single item, to demonstrate that we are not singling out one specific aspect of life.

Still another way to begin would be to look through magazines for pictures that could be used with the teaching picture, "The Children of Israel Worshiping the Golden Calf." Such pictures should be relatively easy to find because almost anything can be made the object of pseudo-religion. As persons arrive, have a few of the earliest arrivals work on making a display that surrounds "The Children of Israel Worshiping the Golden Calf" with present-day portrayals of this picture.

Getting into Things

At the appropriate time you will want to raise the questions, What is idolatry? What is a pseudo-religion?

When the discussion begins, it will be helpful to make use of chapter 2 of *The Decision Maker,* and of Exodus 32:1–6; Daniel 3:1; and

Matthew 6:24, 33. This is also the time to be sure that your group really thinks about the picture, "The Children of Israel Worshiping the Golden Calf." If you have displayed and studied it in the earlier portion of the session, simply call attention to it now. If not, be sure to display it and discuss it now.

The next phase would be the study of chapter 2 of *The Decision Maker*, and Exodus 32:1–6; Matthew 6:24, 33, and the teaching picture. What do these things mean in terms of life today? Is idolatry rampant in *our* lives? If so, in what ways? Is chapter 2 of *The Decision Maker* an authentic portrayal of the tendencies of our basic nature? What kind of vigilance does this require of us?

Concluding the Session

This is the kind of session in which the summary is very important. In the final moments before worship you will want to go over the fact that there really have been two stages in your discussion. (If there have not been two, summarize or have someone else summarize what has happened.)

The first stage was the examination of what the Bible has to say about idolatry. The key to understanding this is the contention of chapter 2 of the resource book: that the Bible really deals more deeply with idolatry than with atheism—that the Bible warns more about the danger of giving supreme loyalty to a false god than about the danger of having no god.

The second stage of this session was the consideration of what idolatry means in terms of our present-day lives. Is idolatry rampant today, as chapter 2 of *The Decision Maker* claims it is?

Looking Ahead

Ask members of the group to study chapter 2 of *The Decision Maker* again in the light of the discussion today, and also to read chapter 3. Ask that they spend some time between this session and the next in studying Exodus 32:1–6 and Matthew 6:24–33. What do these passages mean in terms of our lives today? If members of your group read novels, you might suggest *The Fall*, by Camus, *The Stranger*, by Camus, or *Man in the Gray Flannel Suit*, by Wilson.

Possibilities for Worship

Matthew 6:24–33
Prayer of confession and rededication to the one true God.

Significant but Incomplete

*To the extent that God has a place
in folk religion, he is fundamentally helpmate,
guide, and friend. If God should ever say or do anything
against human interests—although folk religion would be
hard put to conceive of the Divine acting this way—then
so much the worse for God. Any religion inclining
to the view that the divine purpose stands in some
fundamental way in conflict with our purposes
represents superstition or dogmatism or otherworldliness
but not a faith that merits our attention or allegiance.
A mature faith is one which recognizes that God's function
is to conserve and implement human values.*

*Thus, essentially, God is on the side
of people, or, more accurately, he is on the side
of certain persons or a particular community
or a particular nation. He is not necessarily
happy with everyone but he is pleased with those who
are his folk. We demonstrate that we are his folk
by both moral and religious means. On the one hand,
we seek to "lead good, clean lives" and, on the other hand,
we say our prayers, read our Bibles, and attend
church regularly. We are explicitly "religious" in ways that
must be recognized as "good."* [1]

Purpose of This Session

To continue, with a slightly different focus, our exploration of the danger of pseudo-religions. Our purpose in this session is to realize that many of the most significant aspects of life are incomplete when blown up to assume the importance of religions.

Background for the Leader

One of the difficulties about recognizing idolatry is that so many of the things we idolize are of themselves—and in their proper place in life—so meaningful. And, of course, the more significant they are the more temptation there is to worship them. This is true of science, education, and the nation. It is even true of religion.

As you studied and meditated upon the "Thought for the Leader" (above), about what did you think? Did you agree with the comments? Did you react against them?

Actually these paragraphs need a few words of comment to set them into context. The kind of religion described in these paragraphs is really a false religion, a form of the pseudo-religion humanism. The writer uses the phrase "folk religion."

Think about these paragraphs again. Why should we react against the kind of religion portrayed in these words? What is wrong with this kind of religion?

We are not sure whether or not you will want to discuss these paragraphs with your group. If you do you will want to design some way of relating this discussion to that suggested in later sections of this session, in which you make use of a portrait of Christ. Actually the two matters are related, and you may have time to deal with both.

Our major task in this session is to come to realize that it is because these things are so meaningful that we are in danger of making them into idols. This does not mean that they are immoral. It is our nature to make idols of almost anything in life, especially the significant aspects. In order to avoid this tendency we need to remind ourselves that only God is both significant and complete as an object of faith and worship.

It is our suggestion that you make this session more concrete by confining it to one illustration of the truth with which we are dealing. And this one illustration might be made through paintings of Jesus.

JESUS WASHING THE DISCIPLES' FEET   *Fra Angelico*

THE KISS OF JUDAS   *Ravenna, VI Cent.*

Getting Started

For this session you will need some pictures of Jesus. Probably you will have access to at least one large picture. If so, arrange for having it on display during the session. Beneath the picture display the title of this session, "Significant but Incomplete."

There are some pictures of Jesus on page 49 of this coursebook. If you have a large picture, the pictures in this coursebook will be useful later in your discussion. In the event that you are unable to secure a wall picture, you can begin with reference to one of those in the book.

Getting into Things

The contention with which to kick off is that any *one* portrayal of Jesus is idolatrous because it conveys an incomplete even though significant sense of the person of Christ.

One picture may give us the feeling of the humanity of Jesus. Another may give a sense of his divinity. Still another may portray both humanity and divinity, but may not convey the vigor that seems such a prominent aspect of his nature. One picture may give us a sense of his compassion, while a different portrayal may convey the feeling of the severity of his judgment upon our sin. Still another portrayal may movingly convey a sense of his suffering on our behalf.

At this point you will want to study the several pictures of Jesus that are in this coursebook. What impression does each of the various portraits convey? Is any one able to portray the complete personality of Jesus Christ?

Pictures of Jesus can be significant aspects of the Christian life. But it is important to remember that any one picture is unable to give us a complete and living sense of his Sonship and Lordship.

The next phase of this session is to compare with other aspects of life the things that you have learned from your study of this illustration. Just as individual pictures are incomplete portrayals of the person of Jesus, so also such significant parts of life as science, education, the nation, material comforts, human achievements of all sorts, and even the institutional church, are only parts and are not to be set up as ultimate goals in life. (You might skim through chapter 3 of *The Decision Maker*, noticing its headings.) What is the difference between being significant and being complete? How does God fit into life? How is he related to the significant features of life?

Concluding the Session

The concluding phase of this session should be given a rather leisurely treatment. This is because you are striving for understanding and comprehension more than for the transmission of facts. Therefore you might ask several persons to summarize the thinking of the class thus far. What have we been saying, especially during the latter phase of our session? What does this mean for everyday living? If you can secure any kind of a meaningful response to such questions, you will be ending on an extremely significant note.

Looking Ahead

Remind the members of the group that you are now going to move to a different focus on the same side of the paradox of our nature. They key word under discussion will now be sin. Members of the group should study chapter 4 of *The Decision Maker,* entitled "Am I Really a Sinner?"

Possibilities for Worship

Exodus 32:1–6
Prayer of confession
Hymn: "Dear Lord and Father of Mankind"

Additional Resources

You will find useful additional resource material on images of Jesus in an article in the adult section of the March 1964 issue of the *Church School Worker.*

Sins and Sin

> *The point is this. Sin is a religious word.*
> *It defines a man's relationship to God. It is not*
> *primarily moral, like the breaking of customs and laws,*
> *no matter how important they are, any more than faith is*
> *primarily keeping laws and following rules. Neither is sin*
> *primarily bad ethics like wrong behavior at a party*
> *or speaking out unkindly about the new neighbor*
> *next door. Sin is life turning its back on God,*
> *nothing less.*[1]

Purpose of This Session

To explore the meaning of the paradox of man's nature from a slightly altered focus: that we tend to rebel against God by wanting our freedom to be absolutely unlimited; to see how this is sin, as contrasted with sins. This session is based on chapter 4 of the resource book.

Getting Started

One way to begin is to give each person a sheet of paper and ask him to divide it in half by drawing a line down the center. When this is done, request that the left column be given the heading "Sin" and the right column the heading "Sins."

The idea is to dramatize the radical difference between the usual understanding of *sin,* which is "sins," and the deepest biblical understanding, which is "sin"—turning our backs on God. Mention the distinction, and ask that each person really think about the difference (and similarity) by making two lists under the column headings. Allow sufficient time for considerable thought to take place. If persons object that they cannot think of anything to write, ask them just to think about it. Remind them that the value of such an exercise is more in the thought than in the written product.

Getting into Things

As you make your transition to the all-group period of presentation and discussion, you will want to have a chalkboard or sheet of newsprint on which to make lists of examples of "sin" and "sins." Receive and record only enough of the reports to make clear the difference. Perhaps your column of "sin" will consist only of a definition of sin similar to those given in the "Thought for the Leader" at the beginning of this session and the next.

Do not spend too much time on this, because your next task will be to check several Bible passages to discover their concept of sin. For your transition from the receiving of reports to the study of the Bible, say something like: We would all probably like to spend more time on this. But before we do, let's look into the Bible and see what it has to say on this subject.

You may want to read aloud the "Thought for the Leader" with which this session begins, if you have not already done so. Suggest that our Bible study will help us determine the accuracy and truth of this quotation. You may also want to ask someone to read "Sins and Sin" on pages 34–36 of *The Decision Maker.*

There are many passages that could be studied at this time. The two we suggest are Genesis 3:1–7 and Romans 1:18–23. We hope that your group will be able to consider both, either in the kind of small-group study we have previously described, or in general discussion. If you have time for only one passage, however, we suggest it be Genesis 3:1–7, because this is important in relation to Genesis 1, which we will consider later in this unit.

Here are some comments and questions to help in studying these passages. They can be guides for your preparation, or written out as instructions for small study groups.

1. GENESIS 3:1–7. This is part of the second account of creation, which begins at Genesis 2:4b. It is believed to have been written at an earlier time than the account in the first chapter of Genesis. In some ways it gives a more primitive view of God's relation to the world and to man. But it is an extremely important supplement to the "Priestly" account in the first chapter of Genesis because the high status of man in God's plan is not the whole story about man. In this passage we learn of the tendency of man to rebel against living as a creature of God. Man's high destiny under God is thwarted by his rebellion from God and his attempt to be like God.

What is the key verse to the understanding of this passage? Where is the message of this passage "in a nutshell"? (Our vote is for verse 5: "You will be like God.")

What, then, is sin?

Is it true that man is continually trying to put himself in the place of God, or at least in a position of equality with God?

This passage has to do with what theologians call "the fall of man." Does this mean that this is the record of an event that happened once long ago in history? Or should we forget the time element and regard this as an experience in the life of every person? In falling prey to the temptation to play God—judging others, directing the lives of other people, seeking praise, making decisions on the basis only of self-interest—is man not continually falling? (From this question it becomes apparent that we vote with the latter idea: that "the fall of man" is a continuing fact in every man's life.)

2. ROMANS 1:18–23. Which is the key verse in understanding this paragraph? (Our vote is for verse 21: "For although they knew God they did not honor him as God or give thanks to him.")

Does this passage add anything to our understanding of the biblical concept of sin? If so, what?

Note that the "invisible nature" (verse 20) of God, made plain to us in Jesus Christ, is his eternal power and deity. Our sin is our failure to accept God as God. What does this mean?

Concluding and Looking Ahead

We hope that your group will have considerable and lively discussion on the basis of your study of these passages of the Bible and as a result of the above questions about them. If you used small groups, be sure to give opportunity for full expression of opinion as you receive the reports. If your entire group studies the passages together, make certain that you allow sufficient time to raise questions such as those above. In any case, try to give the Bible ample voice.

You will want to say something about the next session. It continues the exploration of the Christian understanding of sin, and concludes the study of one side of the paradox of man's nature: the recurring tendency to rebel against God by trying to be like God, free from all restraint.

The focus is slightly altered in the next session, however. If this is sin, as contrasted with sins, am *I* really a sinner? Is sin universal? If so, how?

Possibilities for Worship

Genesis 3:1–5

Confession of Sin: We suggest the prayer of general confession, page 505 of the *Pilgrim Hymnal,* and page 4 of *The Hymnal* (Evangelical and Reformed).

Hymn: "O Gracious Father of Mankind"

or

Band 2 of *Hymns for Worship—Adult*

Am I Really a Sinner?

*The fundamental definition of sin must be
a religious one, for sin is that which breaks
fellowship with God. It is unbelief. It is willfully
perverting life from God's high destiny. Sin is
an unwillingness to be God's children. It is an insistence
on trying to be God. It is a feverish determination to put
yourself at the center of life and refuse to let God in.
It is a stubborn rebellion against the God who loves you and
formed you to be his own. It is denying your sonship
in "thought, word and deed." Out of all this comes the whole
sordid twist that distorts and discolors life beyond
recognition but never beyond reclaiming.[1]*

Purpose of This Session

To continue our exploration of one side of the paradox of human nature; to focus on the question: In the light of the definition of sin developed in the previous session, am *I* really a sinner?

Getting Started

If you can obtain a recording of Handel's *Messiah,* you might play "All We Like Sheep Have Gone Astray" as persons arrive. Perhaps a soloist could sing it, or could have it recorded on tape.

A helpful way to summarize what has been discussed thus far about the Christian view of man (and an excellent way to recall your last session) would be to make two posters like those reproduced below. You will probably want to do this even if you are able to use the recording mentioned in the preceding paragraph.

MAN'S HIGH STATUS:

RESPONSIBLY FREE

FREEDOM
IN GOD
UNDER GOD !

"LITTLE LESS THAN GOD"
WITH DOMINION OVER ALL
THE REST OF CREATION

MAN'S LOW STATUS:

ENTIRELY FREE

FREEDOM
FROM GOD

"LIKE GOD," NOT
DEPENDENT UPON GOD.
UNLIMITED. TURNING
OUR BACK ON GOD.
"SIN"

As you begin you will want to call attention to the topic and purpose of this session, followed by a presentation (lecture) of a few minutes on the conclusions of your previous session, making clear the distinction between sins and the Bible's deepest concept of sin as turning our backs on God. The posters will be a great asset in this—do not fail to take the time during the week to make them or have them made.

Getting into Things

Then you will want to sharpen the focus of today's session. If sin is as we have been describing it, am I really a sinner? Ask each person silently to review Genesis 3:1–7, paying particular attention to verse 5. After this examine Romans 3:9–12: "All men . . . are under the power of sin, . . . 'None is righteous, no, not one.'" Have each person write this passage in his own words, not using any of the words the Bible uses. Allow ample time for thought and writing. Then hear several of the versions written by members of the group. Do they emphasize the universality of sin? Should they? Is it really true that *all* of us are sinners? If so, in what sense? A major resource for this session is pages 34–36 of the resource book. You may want to have someone read this section. Or you may just want to refer to it, and ask what the members of the group got from it.

For this discussion you might give each member of the group a copy of the confession of sin used most frequently in your church service of worship. Perhaps this would be the prayer of general confession (see suggestions for worship at the conclusion of the preceding session). Is it possible to have a copy of the church hymnal for each person, and to arrange to have these returned in time for use in the church service? If you do not use a prayer of confession in the service, you may want to have copies of such a prayer available. You may want to listen to the Prayer of General Confession in Band 2 of *Hymns for Worship—Adult.*

Should the church service of worship include prayers stating that each one of us is a sinner? Explain. This is another form of the same question: Is sin universal? If sin is defined as we have been defining it, who among us does not sin frequently?

What about the statements on page 40 in the resource book *The Decision Maker?* Is sin involved in each of these statements? If so, in what sense?

Another important question that you might use if time permits is, Are there degrees of sin? Does the idea of degree apply to "sins?" Is there such a thing as degree in the sight of God? Often Christians can be overheard remarking that they "pity" a murderer. In terms of relationship to God, is there a difference in the degree of the sin of the murderer and that of non-murderers?

If time permits, it might be helpful to examine Matthew 19:16–17. What does this say about the universality of sin? ("One there is who is good.")

Concluding and Looking Ahead

A good way to summarize and to conclude would be to point again to the posters with which you began the session. Say a few words about the universality of sin as the Bible conceives of sin, and then summarize the work of the unit thus far, pointing out that we have been stressing one side of the paradox of man. The two posters will guide this presentation. The next two sessions will consider the other side of the riddle that we are: incredible potential! Ask members of the group to prepare for these two sessions by studying chapter 5 of the resource book, entitled "Potential Incredible."

Possibilities for Worship

Jeremiah 17:5–8

If you have the recording of Handel's *Messiah,* play "All We Like Sheep Have Gone Astray."

Silent prayer

or

Band 2 of *Hymns for Worship—Adult*

Another Way to Proceed

On page 36 the resource book states: "He (Jesus) did not practice symptomatic medicine and did not call people to self-contempt or self-condemnation. Instead, in keeping with his own nature and with that of the gospel, he took his hearers to the *cause* of the symptoms and suggested that therapy begin there."

An alternate plan for a portion of this session would relate these statements in the resource book to the question of racial justice. Is racial discrimination *cause* or *symptom?* If symptom, what is the cause? How can and should Christians lead in striving for a healing handling of the treatment of the cause?

The Image of God

*On this important question of the image of God
in man, is there a clear word from God? One fact
is obvious and beyond all dispute: the God of the Christian
revelation is centrally Love, the God of the Cross
and the Resurrection. Simply put, the fact is,
God is faithful.*

*God being Love, his image must be man's capacity
for love. Man is centrally made for love, for God's love
and for man's. The true image includes the truth of all
partial images. Love, for instance, has within it
the reality of* reason, . . . *How can love be high and free
without the power to know, to reflect, to evaluate,
and in the light of this process to choose?* [1]

Purpose of This Session

To explore the extremely high destiny that is part of our endowment; and to focus on the meaning of the word *image*.

Getting Started

This session continues the work of unit II by turning to the other side of the paradox of our nature. In the first portion of the unit the emphasis was on man's tendency toward idolatry and sin. Now we turn to the high destiny and potential of man, created "little less" than God himself. In this session we dig into the meaning of this high destiny by focusing on the meaning of being created in the image of God.

It will be helpful to study Genesis 1:26–31. The second passage suggested for study during this session is Colossians 1:15–20, in which Jesus Christ is definitely acknowledged as "the image of the invisible God" (verse 15).

You will want to explore the meaning of the word *image*. Does it, for example, mean a physical likeness? Or does it mean other qualities? If so, what qualities?

Study the following sentences from *The Interpreter's Bible* to see how they deny the meaning of a physical likeness in favor of "spiritual powers—the power of thought, the power of communication, the power of self-transcendence."

> In view of the fact . . . that in Hebrew thought the body was a part of the whole man and was necessary to his complete being . . . , the representation that man was made "in the image of God" meant much more than that man looked like God or like the divine beings which formed his retinue. The "image" included likeness to them in spiritual powers—the power of thought, the power of communication, the power of self-transcendence.[2]

Also, study again the "Thought for the Leader," and the pertinent portions of chapter 5 of the resource book. Then look at Genesis 1:26–31 and Colossians 1:15–20.

Here is an attempt at expressing the meaning of being created in the image of God. Creation in the image of God does not mean being physically like him. It means sharing his power of loving, of understanding truth, of creating what is beautiful, and of doing what is right. You may want to test some such statement during the discussion period of this session. Read it, at the appropriate time, and ask the group to react to it.

If you are able to put a mirror into the room in which your group meets, you will have a dramatic way of raising the issue. Encourage persons to stand in front of the mirror as they arrive. Either by means of a poster placed beside the mirror, or by standing at the mirror yourself and saying it, ask persons to consider the nature of an image.

If you are unable to get a large mirror, you may be able to obtain a large picture of Jesus or of another person. A poster might ask: Is this an image?

Yet another way of getting started would be to raise the question: How would you represent an image? Have crayons and sheets of newsprint or poster paper (number determined by the size of the group) and ask each person to attempt the representation of an image. If they ask what kind of image, reply that this is precisely what you are asking them.

It would greatly enrich your session if the two key verses of scripture, Genesis 1:26 and Colossians 1:15, were lettered clearly on newsprint or poster paper and mounted where all may see:

HOW WOULD YOU REPRESENT AN IMAGE?

THEN GOD SAID, "LET US MAKE MAN IN OUR IMAGE AFTER OUR LIKENESS."
—GENESIS 1:26

HE [JESUS] IS THE IMAGE OF THE INVISIBLE GOD.
—COLOSSIANS 1:15

Getting into Things

You may be tempted, especially if your group of adults has not been accustomed to such teaching methods, not to take the pains to display these verses of scripture; but we need to consider the fact that most of us remember what we see almost fifty percent better than what we hear!

Your task now is to discuss the meaning of the word *image* on the basis of your study of Genesis 1:26–31, Colossians 1:15–20, and pages 43–57 of the resource book. You may want to use small Bible-study groups (as were suggested in the last session), or you may want to have the entire group look first at one and then at the other of these passages. In either case, here are some questions and comments for consideration.

1. GENESIS 1:26–31. It is interesting to observe the use of the plural rather than the singular for God. "Let *us* make man in *our* image, after *our* likeness." The commentator in *The Interpreter's Bible* says:

> It is evident from [Genesis] 3:22; 11:7; 1 Kings 22:19; Isaiah 6:8, . . . that Hebrew religious thought was familiar with the idea of a heavenly host with whom God took counsel . . . There is thus an echo of polytheism here, but it is only an echo. What seems to be significant is the idea that for the creation of man it was fitting, if not necessary, that there should be something like co-operation on the part of the whole company of heaven.[3]

This is not a major point in your discussion, and you will therefore not want to spend too much time on it. But it may serve to show the high status of man, that the whole company of heaven should have to cooperate in his creation.

Is the image one of physical likeness to God? If not, what kind of likeness to God is meant? Here you may want to try out the statement listed above under "Getting Started" and the "Thought for the Leader," which is a quotation from theologian Nels F. S. Ferré.

Does this kind of likeness give man a high or low status?

If time permits, discuss a question that has been discussed for centuries: Is the image of God in man, or is man in the image of God? Explain.

2. COLOSSIANS 1:15–20. In what sense is Jesus Christ the "image of the invisible God"? Does this mean that in the physical appearance of Jesus Christ we have a "picture" of what God looks like? If not, what kind of "image" of God does Jesus Christ provide? Here too the comments above from "Getting Started" and the "Thought for the Leader" might be of interest. Of this passage, *The Interpreter's Bible* commentator remarks, "As 'image of the invisible God' the Son is God manifest, the bearer of the might and majesty of God, the revealer . . . of the creating and sustaining power" [4] of God. What does this say to our discussion? Does this kind of image give a high or low status to man? How high, or how low?

Summarizing and Looking Ahead

Perhaps in your summary today you will want to indicate that this is by no means an easy subject to discuss. If the group found that man's creation in the image of God does not mean a physical likeness, this should be stressed, and then you may summarize what they think *image* does mean.

Ask the members of the group to consider again chapter 5 of *The Decision Maker* in the light of this session's discussion. This will provide a good basis for discussion at the next session.

Possibilities for Worship

Colossians 1:15–20
Prayer of gratitude for potential
Hymn: "God of Grace and God of Glory"

Potential Incredible

There is darkness in the world,
deep and threatening; only fools pretend there isn't.
There is darkness in our personal lives
even though the masks we wear are bright and smiling.
Our world is out of focus and fragmented. But, for the man
who in a daring, radical act of trust has put his faith
in the brave promises of God, something is coming of it all.
There are streaks of light on the horizon, and little
by little, life is becoming what the New Testament
says it can become, and sings about all the way through—
a long night's journey into day!

I wish that you could get hold of that just the way
I got hold of it once; or, I should say more accurately,
the way it got hold of me. Though I still have
my bad days, though there are still hours when the darkness
closes in, I've never been quite the same since.
It wasn't anything I did really; it's what God did for me,
in Jesus Christ. It's just as the writer of
the Gospel of John says it is: the man who follows Christ
does not have to go stumbling around in the darkness;
he lives his life in the light! [1]

Purpose of This Session

To explore the fact that one aspect of our nature is an incredible potential for godliness and goodness—"little less" than that of God himself! This session is based on chapter 5 of the resource book and on Psalm 8 and Genesis 1:26–31.

Getting Started

If you were able to follow our suggestion and obtain the recording of *The Speak Four Trio,* begin by playing their choral reading of Genesis 1:26–31.

If you do not have the record, there are numerous other possibilities for getting started. You might continue the visualization of the word *image* that we suggested for the previous session. Or you might visualize the word in a different way from those used in your previous session, perhaps using one of the alternate suggestions. (See the suggestions on page 63 of this coursebook.)

Still another way of getting started would be to have a few members of your group do a choral reading of Genesis 1:26–31. This might be presented live or on tape. If you have access to a tape recorder, your group might devote a special session to producing your own choral reading. This could prove to be both enjoyable and educational.

Getting into Things

The heart of this session will be Bible study—preferably in small groups—of Genesis 1:26–31 and Psalm 8. Members of the group should have studied chapter 5 of the resource book during the week. If they have not read this chapter, you may have to include a brief review of it in the class session. Your instructions for small-group Bible study should be carefully prepared and one copy should be available for each small group of not less than three and not more than seven or eight persons. Have some groups study number one while others study number two. How many groups studying each number will be determined by the size of your total group. If your total group is too small to be divided, have everyone study both passages. Your instruction sheets might look like the examples on the following page.

1. STUDY PSALM 8.

Notice that the psalmist is contemplating the heavens at night, for he mentions only the moon and the stars. The "spacious firmament" reminds him of the glory of God.

In the light of this overpowering majesty of God, "what is man?" This is the question to which the psalmist turns in verses 4 and following. What does he say about man?

What is man's destiny? Is it high, or low? How high, or how low? What is his potential? Explain.

What does this say about man's actual status? his purpose? his responsibility?

Do you think that recent scientific discoveries about the universe and about man make the psalmist's views obsolete?

(Be prepared to report your findings to the entire group.)

2. STUDY GENESIS 1:26–31

This account is said to have come from what is called the "priestly" source in the fifth century B.C. However, it reflects a very ancient account of creation and reveals the profound thinking of the Jewish religious leaders in the period following the exile. Remember that it is *not* our purpose to discuss whether or not this is an actual description of the way in which creation took place. This is really beside the point, because the story comes from a time when the methods of scientific investigation and thinking were not yet known. The intention of the writer is to tell of his conviction that the universe is created by God—and in a way that gives man a unique position!

What is man's potential? his status? his purpose? his responsibility?

What is man's position in God's scheme of things? Is his a high, or a low destiny? How high, or how low?

Do you think that recent scientific discoveries about the universe and about man make the author's views obsolete?

If you have time, compare this passage (Genesis 1:26–31) with Genesis 2:4b–9. This latter passage is another account of the creation of man, believed to be an earlier one. Does is say anything about the status and purpose of man? about his responsibility?

(Be prepared to report your findings to the entire group.)

Concluding and Looking Ahead

In summarizing this session and unit II you will want to be sure to maintain a balance of the two sides of the human paradox. Point out that God is the key factor. With him we are incredibly potent; in rebellion against him we falter in sin.

Mention that unit II concludes our exploration of the paradox in our nature—of the riddle that we are. In unit III we turn to the exploration of the Christian heritage. What is the Christian understanding of the nature and purpose of man?

If you have prepared copies of the tentative schedule for unit III, distribute them at this time. If not, read the titles of the sessions in unit III to your group. Ask that they study chapter 6 of the resource book, entitled "Hypocrisy or Despair."

Possibilities for Worship

Band 3, *Hymns for Worship—Adult* (5 minutes)
or
Psalm 8
Hymn: "Ye Servants of God"
Prayer: Gratitude for our incredible potential when we open our hearts to God's love and let him have his way with our lives.

Evaluating

This would be an appropriate time for evaluation. If you are working with a steering committee, arrange for a meeting as soon as possible after the conclusion of the last session of unit II.

SAMPLE OPINION BLANK

We have now completed unit two of our study about man and his purpose in life. The sessions in this unit have concerned the "two sides of the same coin" and have dealt with man as a paradox— his high status under God and in God and his continuing tendency to try to be free from God, which is sin.

1. I have found these sessions to be (check one)
   _____ Decidedly advantageous
   _____ Advantageous
   _____ Fairly helpful
   _____ Of little help
   _____ Quite disappointing

2. I feel that this series of studies contributed something to me by (check one)
   Giving me more information   ____Yes ____No
   Changing my attitudes   ____Yes ____No
   Changing my life   ____Yes ____No

3. What was the most helpful? _____

   _____

4. What was your biggest disappointment? _____

   _____

5. What needs clarification or additional treatment? _____

   _____

6. I would like to see the group discuss the following: _____

   _____

7. Other comments: _____

   _____

   _____

Unit III
EXPLORING THE CHRISTIAN HERITAGE

Unit III is a six- or seven-session unit that explores the Christian heritage on the subject of man's nature and purpose in life, especially that part of the heritage that is recorded in the Bible. In this unit we ask ourselves, "In the light of the riddle that we are, what does Christianity have to say?"

If you need to combine two sessions in order to reduce the unit to six sessions, we suggest that you combine sessions III–6 and III–7.

Session III–1, "The Need for Recurring Rescue," recalls unit II, reminding us of Christianity's conviction that our puzzling human nature is in constant need of a Power greater than ourselves. This session is based on the early portions of chapter 6 of the resource book, and leads us to recognize that God always takes the initiative in effecting the ever–necessary reunion.

"The Difference Between the Covenants," session III–2, disallows the common misconception that the Old Testament is based on law and the New Testament on love. It claims that both the Old Testament and the New Testament are based on both law and love, and stresses the fact that Jesus Christ is the difference between the covenants. He is our Rescuer or Redeemer.

Session III–3 delves into the Old Covenant and its outgrowth, the law. It finds that the law makes major contributions to our lives, but has severe limitations when miscast in the role of redeemer. In such a role it leads either to hypocrisy or to despair.

Session III–4 stresses the fact that it is "Love that Fulfills the Law," especially the love incarnate in Jesus. It suggests the use of a play.

"Redemption in Love," session III–5, continues the exploration of the nature of Christian love. It sees Christian love as redemptive or reuniting love. It examines the good news that God accepts the unacceptable.

Session III–6 balances the previous session with an emphasis upon the justice in love. Redemptive love is at the same time just. Far from being soft or impractical, it is the very substance of life—the most potent force in the world.

The final session, III–7, takes note of the fact that Christian love has a vital tension. It also leads us to thank God for the good news of redemption and forgiveness.

THE CRUCIFIED CHRIST   *Georges Rouault*

The Need for Recurring Rescue

So long as there is history, God will be at work
with the wrongness of life, coming to grips constantly
with powers and principalities, with the wretched, stubborn,
egotistical selves of men which stand so defiantly
under the arches of heaven. You know that he will
because of the way he acted once out of his own free will,
in his own peculiar way, with his own life.
It is just that life which makes the atonement, which stands
in promise all across the future, all up and down the past—
not the things you say about it, not the teachings
many people try to cut loose from it. It is that very life
carrying off so gallantly, even now, all the sin
and utter chaos of life and winning over it all.
The atonement is this truth made real
in the life of a Person.[1]

Purpose of This Session

To show that our paradoxical nature leaves us in need of recurring rescue by a Power greater than ourselves; and to recognize that God always takes the initiative in this reconciliation.

Background for the Leader

This session is based on pages 58 to 73 of the resource book, *The Decision Maker*. You will want to return to the resource book and study these pages carefully. The session is also based on the study of 2 Corinthians 5:16–21; Luke 18:9–14; and Romans 8:3–4.

This session recalls unit II. If our paradoxical nature is such that we tend to thwart our incredible potential by rebelling against dependency upon God, we are in the position of needing rescue—recurring rescue, time and time again. By our playing God we put distance between God and ourselves. We are estranged. We need a Power greater than ourselves to restore the relationship. We are unable to effect this reconciliation with God that we so earnestly desire. God always takes the initiative in restoring the fellowship. Theologians have long said that God achieves atonement, a theological word that means exactly what the word says. God takes the initiative in bringing about at-one-ment with him, in restoring our ruptured relationship.

Getting Started

We would begin by having a question posted on the wall, written on the chalkboard, or typed on individual slips of paper: "If we are all sinners, what does it mean to say that we all stand in need of recurring rescue?" You may want to suggest the use of pages 59 to 62 of *The Decision Maker* as resource material.

When members of the group have had enough time to think over this question, you may want to begin the discussion by reminding them that the first step into an effective involvement in Alcoholics Anonymous is that you must publicly admit your inability to control yourself—your need of a power greater than yourself. A very similar situation applies in the Christian religion. The beginning point is the recognition and admission that we are not able to be the captains of our own souls. We stand in need of a Power greater than ourselves. Do we really believe this? If we believe intellectually, do we believe it in our daily living?

Getting into Things

We would approach this portion of the session with the use of small-group Bible study. If the group is large enough, why not divide into two or more small groups of six or seven persons each, with some groups studying some of the following suggestions and other groups studying others? If your group is small, you can divide into groups of three or four persons each, or you can study these passages with your group as a whole.

1. LUKE 18:9–14. In this parable of the pharisee and the publican what do you think is the one main point? Do you think it says anything about man's ability to achieve his own reconciliation with God? In this regard, pay particular attention to verses 9 and 14. Do you think we really need "rescue" or "salvation"? If so, do we need this only one time during our pilgrimage on earth, or many times?

2. 2 CORINTHIANS 5:16–21. What does this passage seem to say about man's being reconciled with God? What is a "new creation," and who creates it? Give especially extensive attention to verse 19. What does this say? How would you express it in your own words? Do you think we really need reconciliation at the hands of God? If so, must he do this for us only one time, or on numerous occasions?

3. ROMANS 8:3–4. In modern, everyday English, what do you think these verses mean? Do you agree with Paul? Do we really need what God does for us? If so, do we need this once during our lifetime, or on numerous occasions?

What this session really does is to ask us whether we really believe that the result of sin is alienation from God, and the loss of our ability to do good and to love God and our fellowmen. Do we really believe that we have any need for a Power greater than ourselves? It is hoped that any discussion of this question will involve not only an answer with our lips but also a serious consideration of how we answer this with our daily lives. Also, is this something which happens once during a lifetime, or frequently? Finally, do we really believe that God must reach down and pick us up, or do we still feel that through our own efforts we can pull ourselves up?

Concluding the Session

You will probably have an excellent summary of this session if you are able to draw together the ideas of the group on the above three questions. At any rate, you might stress the point that the Christian religion is much more concerned with the nature of God than the nature of man. Any study of the nature of man must inevitably lead us to the good news that God fills and fulfills our life. The gospel is God-centered, not man-centered.

With this in mind we have suggested for worship the hymn "Praise Ye the Father for His Lovingkindness" or the hymn in band 3 of *Hymns for Worship—Adult,* both of which express our thanksgiving to the God who rescues us recurringly.

You will want to point ahead to the next session, which explores the contention that Jesus Christ is the one who rescues or redeems us. He is God's new covenant, and is the difference between the old covenant and the new. Remind the group that the next session will be based on chapter 7 of *The Decision Maker.*

Possibilities for Worship

Band 3 of *Hymns for Worship—Adult*
or
2 Corinthians 5:16–21
Hymn: "Praise Ye the Father for His Lovingkindness"
Prayer

Christt: the Difference Between the Covenants

With Christ's coming, the image of God in man became filled by being fulfilled. . . . Christ showed man the perfect will of God and the mature nature of man. Christ showed man his right relation to God.

God reduced in Christ the laws of the Old Testament decalogue to two: love to God and love to man, universal and entire. This concentration of the ten into two commands had already been accomplished by Judaism; Jesus himself had been brought up reciting them daily.

But in Jesus these two laws became demonstrated in life as well as explicated in meaning. In Jesus, too, the law of perfect love became, beyond every command, the Gospel of God's grace. The law of love became fulfilled in the life of Love.[1]

Purpose of This Session

To disallow the common misconception that the Old Testament (covenant) is based on law and the New Testament (covenant) on love. To explore the way in which the difference between the covenants (both based on both law and love) is Jesus Christ. He is the Redeemer, the Rescuer, the Reconciler!

Background for the Leader

The Christian heritage portrays Jesus Christ as the Redeemer. The idea of this session is to help adults to realize that even as we talk about how we need recurring rescue, this rescue is accomplished by Jesus Christ.

You may attain a deeper realization of this fact by thinking through the covenant idea. The resource book, on pages 65 to 73, tells about the meaning of the word *covenant* and about the historical development of the covenant. You will want to study these pages carefully.

Jesus is the difference between the covenants because he does the rescuing that we cannot do for ourselves, thereby opening up the possibility of our achieving more of our incredible potential than we had ever thought possible.

Getting Started

This session is based on pages 75–78 and on chapter 7 of *The Decision Maker,* and on the following Bible passages: Deuteronomy 6:4–6; Leviticus 19:18; Matthew 5:17; Romans 13:10. You could make good use of the teaching picture from Audio-Visual Packet 1, "The Last Supper" by Fra Angelico, and, if it is available, the aria from Handel's *Messiah,* "I Know That My Redeemer Liveth." (If you cannot secure the record you might have a local soloist record this selection on tape.)

We suggest that you have a record player or tape recorder playing "I Know That My Redeemer Liveth" as people arrive for the session and that you have your reproduction of the masterpiece "The Last Supper" set up at the front of the room. For your purposes in this session you might put up beside it a poster with the words "The New Covenant in His Blood." You might also display a poster bearing these two questions: (1) What is a redeemer? (2) Who is our Redeemer?

Getting into Things

Below are a few key questions for getting into discussion on this theme, either in small groups or in your group as a whole.

What is a covenant? (As you raise this question, it might be helpful to ask members of the group to open to the beginning of the Old Testament or New Testament in their Bibles. Some of them will undoubtedly have a title page reading "The Old Covenant, commonly called the Old Testament," or "The New Covenant, commonly called the New Testament." Helps for discussing the meaning of a covenant will be found in the resource book and in Bible dictionaries. Study pages 65–68 of the resource book.)

Is the old covenant based on law, or love?

Is the new covenant based on law, or love?

Is the old covenant based primarily on what God does, or on what man achieves for himself? What about the New Testament?

Is the New Testament based on the spirit or on the letter of the law? (See 2 Corinthians 3:6.)

Concluding the Session

At this point you might read and discuss the meaning of Hebrews 9:11–22. As you do so, you will want to make use of the teaching picture for this session, and discuss the meaning of the word *redeem*. What is redemption? Who is our redeemer?

This will give you a very natural way of summarizing this session. In your summary you will want to emphasize the point that both covenants are based on both law and love, and that the difference between the covenants is Jesus Christ. He is the Redeemer, the Rescuer! He is the New Covenant, through the pouring out of his blood. This is the good news of the Last Supper.

You will want to inform the group that the next session will take up the positive contributions as well as the inadequacies of the law, based on chapter six of *The Decision Maker*.

Possibilities for Worship

Band 4 of *Hymns for Worship—Adult* (3 minutes)
or
Hebrews 9:11–22
Hymn: "Crown Him with Many Crowns"
Prayer

The Old Covenant and the Law

*God's law in the covenant was not conceived as
a penal burden to be borne. It was God's gracious gift
to Israel that the nation, which previously had lived
outside the benefits of law, might now know the security
which is derived from justice. It was not an invention of men;
it was the expression of the authoritative will
of the covenant God.*[1]

Purpose of This Session

To discover how the Old Covenant, though initiated by God, depended upon man's ability to live up to God as the law revealed him; to note the contribution of the law to the Christian life, as well as its inadequacies.

Getting Started

This is a session on the contribution of the law to the Christian life, especially taking note of its inadequacies. Early arrivals might be encouraged to compare the ten commandments, as recorded either in Exodus 20 or Deuteronomy 5, with the fragment of the Covenant Code in Exodus 34:10–26. You might prepare written instructions to this effect, noting that comment on this matter is on pages 65–67 of the resource book, *The Decision Maker*. If any persons have time enough to make a real comparison, you might begin the group session with a brief report on their research. In your preparation for this session, devote a considerable portion of your time to the study of pages 65–73 of *The Decision Maker*.

Getting into Things

Three large questions form the heart of this session. You might want the entire group to consider them in turn, or have small groups take one question each, study it, and report to the entire group.

1. Is the law binding for Christians? Study Matthew 5:17. What do you think this means to the life of a present-day Christian?

2. What is the most important role or roles of law in the Christian life? See the resource book, page 69, and Galatians 3:19–29 or Romans 7:7–12. What do you think this means to the life of a present-day Christian?

3. When and why is the law limited? See the resource book, page 70, and Galatians 3:19–29 or Romans 7:7–12. What do you think this means to the life of a present-day Christian?

If you choose to have small study-groups, be sure to have additional copies of the questions ready so that a group that finishes one question may continue with the next without waiting for the others. Or, if they have not already done so, you may want to ask them to consider the comparison suggested under the section above, "Getting Started."

Concluding the Session

Is there enough agreement among members of the group so that you can formulate some conclusions? If so, what are they? If not, should there be? Is the resource book true to the Scriptures in its portrayal of both the contribution and the limitation of the law?

As a means of looking ahead, you might mention that we have now explored the difference between the old covenant and the new covenant, have found that both are based on both law and love, and that Jesus Christ, the difference between the two covenants, is our Redeemer and Rescuer! In the next session we enter into an exploration of the manner or method of the Redeemer. In what way is "love the fulfilling of the law"? This session will be based on chapter 8 of the resource book.

If you are planning to use the skit suggested for the next session, you will want copies available at this session so that you can recruit persons to portray the roles. Make it clear that this is not to be a polished presentation, but an attempt to feel the impact of the discussion.

Possibilities for Worship

Matthew 5:17, Galatians 3:19–29 or Romans 7:7–12
Hymn: "Rock of Ages"
Prayer: Gratitude for the law and its positive role, and a petition for its fulfillment in love

Love That Fulfills the Law

*Who can describe the [blessed] bond
of the love of God? What man is able to tell the excellence
of its beauty, as it ought to be told? The height
to which love exalts is unspeakable. Love unites us to God.
Love covers a multitude of sins. Love beareth all things,
is long-suffering in all things. There is nothing base,
nothing arrogant in love. Love admits of no schisms:
love gives rise to no seditions: love does all things
in harmony. By love have all the elect of God
been made perfect; without love nothing is well-pleasing to God.
In love has the Lord taken us to Himself. On account
of the Love he bore us, Jesus Christ our Lord
gave His blood for us by the will of God; His flesh
for our flesh, and His soul for our souls.*[1]

Purpose of This Session

To explore the Redeemer's method; to make a beginning at trying to understand Christian love.

Getting Started

For this session we suggest imagining that you are a theater group producing a play entitled "The Redeemer's Method"—A Play in One Act. We suggest that you arrange your chairs like a theater, either in the round or in a more conventional shape, and that you prepare a mimeographed program which will be distributed by ushers. As people arrive, have a phonograph playing "I Know That My Redeemer Liveth," from Handel's *Messiah;* or a tape recorder can be playing this music—recorded in advance by a soloist or organist.

The program that one group prepared is reproduced at the conclusion of our suggestions for this session. The program is reproduced on page 86, and the text of the skit appears on pages 86–88. The cover of the program consisted of construction paper with a cross pasted on it. Probably someone in your group would thoroughly enjoy making these. If not, you may want to have bulletin covers, available from the United Church Bookstores, or a mimeographed cover with an original design.

Getting into Things

"A Word from the Prompter" is your opportunity to greet people and to review the results of the previous session, as well as to introduce the purpose of this presentation. You may want to mention that the method of the Redeemer was not at all what most people expected, and that the real meaning of love is not commonly understood today because of the many meanings attached to the word *love.* Christian love is redemptive love. The next few sessions will be used for the exploration of the Christian understanding of love, the Redeemer's method.

The skit on pages 86–88 is what one group used for this session. You may want to write one of your own; or your group could role-play this situation.

Following the skit we suggest that you devote a few minutes to the discussion of the kind of love portrayed in the skit. You may want to examine Matthew 5:43–48, or sections of the resource book which deal with this subject.

"A Word from the Actors" is the cue for discussion, indicating that in the Christian religion everyone is in the "play." There is no passive audience. All are "actors."

Concluding the Session

For this session your summary will probably seek only to point out that the Redeemer's method is "love," a word with much deeper meanings than is often realized. You may also want to announce that in the next session the group will delve even more deeply into the meaning of Christian love by attempting to understand the element of *redemption* in love!

Ask everyone to be sure to study chapter 8 of the resource book and Matthew 20:1–16 for the purpose of discovering what is the one main point of the parable.

Another Way to Proceed

If you choose not to use the skit recommended here, you may prefer to make this session a study of the parable of the laborers in the vineyard (Matthew 20:1–16). In this case you might well make use of some of the suggestions and comments given in the next session (session 5 of unit III). We believe that there is more than enough material in session 5 for two sessions.

Possibilities for Worship

Matthew 5:43–48
Hymn: "Immortal Love, Forever Full"
Prayer: Gratitude for the depth of Christian love, confession for the glibness of our treatment of it, and petition for a deeper concern for its true nature

Additional Resources

Among the best additional resources are the writings of Reuel L. Howe. The book that deals most directly with love is *Herein Is Love*. Perhaps you will be able to borrow a copy from your church library, from the public library, or from your pastor.

But there is much on this subject in the other books by Reuel L. Howe. If you are able to obtain copies of the following books, study them for help on this subject: *Man's Need and God's Action* and *The Miracle of Dialogue*.

Welcome to our performance of—
THE REDEEMER'S METHOD
A one-act play exploring Christian love

MUSICAL PRELUDE: From the *Messiah,* including "I Know That My Redeemer Liveth"

A WORD FROM THE PROMPTER: *Introduction*

CHARACTERS (*in order of appearance*):

Sam

Mrs. Anderson

Mr. Anderson

Trudy

SETTING: *As the scene opens we find the Andersons gathered in the living room. They have had dinner, and the dishes are finished. Mrs. Anderson is doing some mending, while Mr. Anderson is reading the evening paper. He is wearing slippers and a lounging robe. Sam, sixteen, and Trudy, fourteen, are working on crossword puzzles.*

THE PLAY: "The Redeemer's Method"

A WORD FROM THE ACTORS (including *you*): Discussion of the idea that redemption is through acceptance of the unacceptable, and that unearned (Christian) love depends on the initiative of the giver rather than the merit of the recipient.

The Redeemer's Method [2]
A Play in One Act

SAM: Mom, how do you spell "embarrass"? With one *r* or two?

MRS. ANDERSON: With two, I think, Sam. But I'm not sure. You'd better ask your father.

MR. ANDERSON (*without looking up*): Two is right.

(*Sam and Trudy work quietly for a minute or so.*)

TRUDY: Why is it that you always do better than I do? I get along all right when I'm working on puzzles with some of the girls at school. But you always seem to be so lucky when we work on puzzles here at home.

SAM: Now, wait a minute, Trudy! It's not just a matter of being lucky. After all, it *does* take some skill to do crossword puzzles.

TRUDY: Well, you are two years older than I am. But I still think that I can spell better than you can.

SAM: What makes you think so?

TRUDY: Those letters from camp last summer. The spelling was atrocious!

SAM: Oh, I was in a hurry when I wrote those. Besides they weren't as bad as all that.

MRS. ANDERSON (*breaking in*): For heaven's sake you two. Can't you ever work on crossword puzzles without getting into an argument?

SAM: Sorry, Mom. (*Sam and Trudy now work quietly for a moment. Mr. Anderson breaks the silence.*)

MR. ANDERSON: Here's a strange story. It's about a man who has just been released from prison after serving a one-year term. It seems he was arrested when his employer discovered that for years he had been stealing from the company's warehouse. The other day when he was released, his employer was there to greet him. He drove him back to his home and told him that he was to report for work the next day. His old job was waiting for him. In addition, when the man was reunited with his family he learned that his employer had been paying his wages in full to his wife all the time he had been in prison.

SAM: Boy, that *is* a strange story! Don't you think the employer is taking a terrible risk in letting the guy have his job back, Dad?

MR. ANDERSON: I doubt it, Sam. I should think it would be very difficult for that man ever to steal from his employer again. I know that if someone were to treat *me* that way, I would be so thankful that all the rest of my life I would do my best to show him how much I appreciated it.

MRS. ANDERSON: I agree with that, but I'm wondering what part the employer played in the man's trial. Perhaps if he had taken the stand in his behalf, testified to his good character, and promised to take him back, it would not even have been necessary for the man to go to prison at all. Does the paper say what stand the employer took when the man was arrested?

MR. ANDERSON: Yes, it says that he testified for the prosecution. He described the nature of the crime and the relationship that he had had with the employee in the past. Apparently he trusted the man completely.

TRUDY: But the guy did something wrong, Mom. I think that he *should* have gone to prison.

MRS. ANDERSON: I suppose so, Trudy. And I suppose that if he had not had to suffer for his crime and had been forgiven so easily, he might have started stealing again. As things are now, he has discovered that the employer is really his friend, and he probably feels deeply indebted to him.

SAM: You know, I'm wondering what I would have done in that employer's situation. I'm afraid that I would have washed my hands of him. If anyone treated me that way after I had trusted him, I think I would have left him take what was coming to him.

MR. ANDERSON: Well, you know, Sam, I too am not sure what I would have done. But I have a pretty good idea what I *ought* to have done. I think that merchant must be a Christian, because it seems to me that what he did is a pretty good example of what we mean when we talk about God's love. It's a love that is neither soft and spineless on the one hand, nor legalistic on the other. The man experienced the consequences of his wrongdoing, but was forgiven. And it was a *creative* forgiveness, because it brought him into a new relationship with his employer. And you know, that kind of love is not cheap. It would have been easier simply to fire the man and forget about him or to overlook the man's stealing—saying that all was forgiven—and allowing him to go on working as though nothing had happened. Instead the employer had the man arrested and punished by due process of law. But he paid his salary while he was in jail, kept his job open for him, and ran the risk of criticism and loss of business for rehiring a man with a prison record.

SAM: I never thought about Christian love in that way, Dad. I sort of thought that God's love for us was entirely different from the kind of love *we* can show. But now I'm not so sure. The man in that article forgave the worker, just as God forgives us, even when we do not deserve it. In a way, that seems irresponsible and sort of foolish. How can such a God be called a *just* God? Shouldn't a person be required to do something to prove he is worthy before he is forgiven? It seems to me *that* would be justice! But if God treated *us* like that, there wouldn't be much chance for us, would there?

Redemption in Love

All too commonly, love is regarded as a sentiment,
a feeling, a "liking" for someone.
While sentiment and emotion are certainly a part of love,
it is tragic to make them synonymous with love.
Certainly we mean more than that when we say,
"God is love," or when we wrestle with
the concept of man showing his love
of God through his love for his neighbor.
In these concepts we are thinking of love as the moving,
creating, healing power of life;
of love that is "the moving power of everything
toward everything else that is." Love reunites life with life,
person with person, and as such is not easily discouraged.
. . . We are called to love one another
reunitingly with the love wherewith God loved us.[1]

Purpose of This Session

To continue our effort to understand Christian love; to consider the nature of *redemptive* love; to hear the good news of how God accepts the unacceptable and loves even those who do not merit his love.

Getting Started

As persons arrive, ask each to write his answer to the question: How would you describe *Christian* love? You might post the question on newsprint, write it on a chalkboard, or have it typed on individual sheets of paper with blank space for the answer. Suggest pages 87–95 of *The Decision Maker* as resource material for study in responding to this question.

Getting into Things

Because it is important in this session to be sure to delve deeply in our search for understanding Christian or redemptive love (love for the unlovable), we suggest that you divide your group into small discussion groups of not less than three and not more than six or seven persons each. We suggest that you prepare instructions for each group in advance. Below are suggestions for instructions for three groups.

1. STUDY MATTHEW 20:1–16.

What is the one main point of this parable?

Which is the key verse in understanding this parable?

On the basis of this parable, how would you define Christian, or redemptive, love?

(This is a parable about the nature of God. The good news of the gospel is that he is the kind of God who accepts his children not on the basis of their merits but out of the goodness of his own heart. That is the one main point of the parable. Most commentators seem to feel that the key verse in understanding the parable is not 16 but 15: "Am I not allowed to do what I choose with what belongs to me? Or do you begrudge my generosity?")

Does our church love redemptively? Our community?

If time permits, compare Matthew 20:1–16 to Matthew 5:43–48. What additional insights does this yield? Or examine John 13:34. What about this?

2. STUDY JOHN 13:31–35. Notice especially John 13:34:

"A new commandment I give to you, that you love one another; even as I have loved you, that you also love one another."

How has Jesus Christ loved us? How does he love us?

It is recorded that when he was on the cross Jesus prayed for his murderers: "Father, forgive them; for they know not what they do" (Luke 23:34). What does this say about the way in which he loved us?

What kind of love does this demand of us? How would you describe redemptive, or Christian love?

Does our church love redemptively? our community?

If time permits, compare this passage to Matthew 5:43–48. What additional insights does this yield?

3. STUDY MATTHEW 5:43–48.

What kind of love is Jesus describing here? On the basis of this passage and of your other study of the Christian religion, how would you describe Christian or redemptive love?

Does our church love redemptively? our community?

If time permits, compare this passage to John 13:31–35. What additional insights does this yield?

Concluding the Session

Your remaining time could probably best be used in a general discussion of how the group would describe Christian love, based on the small-group Bible study that has preceded it. How did your groups answer their questions? What conclusions can be agreed upon by the total group?

Possibilities for Worship

Band 4, *Hymns for Worship—Adult* (3 minutes)

Justice in Love

*Cheap grace is the preaching
of forgiveness without requiring repentance,
baptism without church discipline, Communion without
confession, absolution without contrition.
Cheap grace is grace without discipleship, grace without
the Cross, grace without Jesus Christ, living and incarnate.*

*Costly grace is the treasure hidden in the field.
. . . It is costly because it costs a man his life, and it is
grace because it gives a man the only true life. . . .
It is* costly *because it cost God the life of his Son:
. . . and what has cost God much cannot be cheap for us.
Above all, it is* grace *because God did not reckon his Son
too dear a price to pay for our life, but delivered him
up for us. Costly grace is the Incarnation of God.*[1]

Purpose of This Session

This session is based on pages 94–105 of the resource book and on Matthew 25:31–46; John 14:15–24; and Matthew 5:17–20. Its purpose is to balance the emphasis on redemption in love with an equally strong emphasis on justice in love; to learn that, far from being "soft" and impractical, redemptive love is the basic essence of life.

Getting Started

The prevalent contention that Christian love is soft and impractical, that it has no concern and passion for justice, simply is not valid when the word *love* is adequately defined. John McIntyre, in his book *On the Love of God,* speaks to this situation:

> If we are thus seriously going to restore the theme of the love of God to its central position in the message of the Church, we must be on our guard against turning the wheel of history backwards to the Liberal message of the thirties, or earlier. Grim things have happened in the interval, things that crowded out for many the possibility of this subject. In re-stating it, therefore, we must keep constantly in mind the circumstances which seemed to silence this message. . . . *else we return to the old optimism and shallowness from which we had hoped to escape,* and which events of modern history had called into question.[2]

In subsequent chapters of this excellent book, the author goes on to consider Christian love as concern, commitment, communication, community, involvement, identification, response and responsibility. A careful and thoughtful consideration of this list should help us to see that Christian love is the most just and most potent, most spiritually dynamic, force known to man.

This session should lead your group to the consideration of the firmness, the dynamic force, and the justice in redemptive love. Needless to say, it will call for careful and prayerful preparation on your part. Study pages 94–105 of the resource book, the "Thought for the Leader," McIntyre's quotation, and the biblical passages mentioned in the "Purpose for This Session."

To get started, you may want to refer back to the skit in session 4, if you used it. In this case the question to raise would be whether or not the conduct of the employer toward the employee was just, and if so, why.

You will probably want to have on hand a copy of the skit, so that at the appropriate time you can read the section where it says that the employer testified for the prosecution at the trial, and described the nature of the crime and the employer-employee relationship.

If you did not use the skit, you may want to describe the situation to the group in your own words and have a discussion of the issues involved. Or you may want to use one of the situations described on pages 90 and 91 of *The Decision Maker*. Ask, Is there any kind of justice in such love? If so, what kind?

In any case, the important question, on which this entire session is built is, What is the relationship of love and justice?

Our opinion on the matter (and, we hope, some resource material for your use) is in the resource book sections entitled "The Justice in Love" and "The Tension in Love," (pages 94–95 of *The Decision Maker*).

Getting into Things

After some discussion of the opinions of the group, you might well suggest turning to the Word of God for enlightenment. We suggest the study of three passages of the Bible: Matthew 25:31–46, the parable (or vision) of the last judgment; John 14:15–24, a call for the keeping of the commandments as an integral part of love; and Matthew 5:17–20, a call for righteousness that exceeds that of the scribes and Pharisees.

If your group is small you may look at each of the passages in turn, or you might ask one or two persons to study each of the passages. If your group is large, you may either take one or two passages in turn (eliminating Matthew 5:17–20 if time does not permit), or you might divide into small groups, each group to consider one passage. In every case the big question is, What is the relationship of love and justice?

If the discussion lags, or if you want to call the attention of the group back from Bible principles to Christian practice, you might recall the skit of session 4 or an incident or two from pages 90 and 91 of the resource book. In case you do this, be certain to bring the Bible principles that you have just studied into your discussion of the Christian practice in such life situations. What does the Bible have to do, for instance, with loving a disagreeable neighbor?

Concluding and Looking Ahead

What is the relationship of love and justice? Is there general agreement among the members of the group? If not, does Christian truth demand agreement? What? Is the opinion expressed on pages 94 and 95 of *The Decision Maker,* true to the Scriptures? What does it all mean?

If your schedule permits the use of the coming session on "The Tension in Love," look forward to this by calling the attention of the group to the fact that this will conclude the third unit. If not, be sure to include something about tension in love in your plans for this session, as well as some way of concluding unit 3.

Possibilities for Worship

Scripture: John 14:15–24
Hymn: "Make Me a Captive, Lord"
Prayer: Gratitude for the fullness of the love of God, which is
    never overly optimistic or shallow, but realistic and full.

Tension in Love

*It is important to emphasize that the two sides
of the experience of grace are so related that they
do not contradict, but support each other. To understand
that the Christ in us is not a possession but a hope,
that perfection is not a reality but an intention;
that such peace as we know in this life is never purely the
peace of achievement but the serenity of being "completely
known and all forgiven"; all this does not destroy
moral ardour or responsibility. On the contrary
it is the only way of preventing premature completions
of life, or arresting the new and more terrible pride
which may find its roots in the soil of humility,
and of saving the Christian life from the intolerable
pretension of saints who have forgotten that they are sinners.[1]*

Purpose of This Session

To conclude and summarize our thoughts and feelings about the nature and implications of redemptive love; to strive for balance of tensions in our understanding; to thank God for the good news of redemption and forgiveness.

Getting Started

This session does not advance any new information, but is designed for summarizing and concluding both your study of redemptive love and of the whole of unit III, which is an exploration of our Christian heritage to discover its view of man and his nature.

One way to get started would be to display on a poster or on the chalkboard the request that each person on arriving write a description or definition of *grace*. If you use this approach, have paper and pencils ready for those who do not bring their own.

Depending upon how much time you want to give to this phase of the session, you may want to add such questions as this to your poster:

What is meant by redemption?

What is redemptive love?

How can love be just and also redemptive?

An alternate way to get started would be to ask the members of your group to meditate silently upon Psalm 51. We suggest that this psalm be the heart of your worship for this session.

Getting into Things

In this session you should be concerned not so much about new information as about expression and discussion of opinions. Your group ought to have an animated and enlightening discussion of the group's overall understanding of the fact that redemptive love involves justice. It is difficult not to slide to one side or the other. Are you sure that in your previous session's emphasis on justice in love your group did not all but negate the dynamic and seemingly foolish nature of redemption in love? On the other hand, is your understanding of redemptive love such that it includes a creative sense of firmness and justice? Your discussion should revolve around the *tension* in love. What are the elements of this tension? How do they express themselves in modern-day life? What does it mean to

love redemptively in our church? in our community? in our homes? See the "Thought for the Leader." It is worth studying in class.

Do not be concerned if there are moments of silence during this session. Deep and vitally significant thought may be taking place. In fact, this session probably should move at a very leisurely pace. It is a time for thinking back, for self-examination, and for pledging ourselves (in the silence of our hearts) to put redemptive love to work in church, in community, in home. It is a time to marvel about the wonder of it all—love by which God accepts me into his presence, right here and now, just as I am, without any strings attached. And accepts me, no matter to what depths I have fallen. No matter what!

Concluding and Looking Ahead

More than the usual time should be allowed for summarizing and concluding. In fact, you may want to make this another occasion for using an opinion blank or evaluation form similar to those suggested earlier in the course. In any case, be sure to "wrap up" and review some of the highlights of the unit and especially this study of redemptive love. If you have had someone keeping notes of the high points, by all means call for a report. If not, be sure to take the time, rather leisurely, to look backward and to review the progress of the group thus far.

Possibilities for Worship

We suggest that your closing worship be built around Psalm 51. You may want to have someone read the entire psalm. Or two or three persons might read it as a scriptural speech drama. They could do so by reading alternate verses and at high points (such as verses 3, 10, 15, and 17) all reading in unison. This would, of course, require their getting together in advance for practice. If you desire to sing a hymn we suggest "Joyful, Joyful, We Adore Thee." After singing the hymn, why not use its words as your prayer?

After the Session

If you have a steering committee (as suggested and described on page 20) it should meet as soon as possible after this session for a look backward (evaluation) and a look forward (planning).

If you have not appointed a steering committee, ask several persons to meet with you for a brief discussion of the progress of the course and of possible future activities and emphases.

Unit IV
EXPLORING
THE CHALLENGE

This is the concluding unit of five sessions dealing with our response to the challenge in the Christian heritage. In unit III we explored the Christian heritage. In this final unit we examine the nature of our responsibility and opportunity.

If you must combine two sessions in order to reduce this unit to four sessions, we suggest that you combine sessions IV–3 and IV–4.

Unit IV delves into the decision of our lives about our response to the kind of love with which God loves us, and explores the role of our day-by-day decisions in designing a style of life in which we live maturely in freedom—in captivity to the Spirit.

Session IV–1 reflects unit III's closing emphasis on the kind of love that God is. In response to what was uncovered in this exploration in unit III, we begin this unit with the question "Can I Love as Christ Does?" We learn that we can love as Christ does, but imperfectly. Perfection in this kind of love is what we are always striving toward. It ever remains our intention.

The second session of the unit continues in the same vein. It considers what is involved in growing in grace. It sees growth in grace as "The Process of Gratitude"—a process that never ends. "Thought for the Leader" at the head of this session stresses the fact that growth in grace confronts us with a task of immense proportion.

Session IV–3 focuses on what is involved as a result of the fact that God gives us our salvation as a gift that takes a lifetime to accept and appropriate. Our process of growing in grace is characterized by freedom—but Christians recognize that freedom is genuine only when it is in captivity to God. This session explores the beginning portions of chapter 10 of *The Decision Maker*.

"Responsible Decision-Making" is what results from our freedom in captivity. This is the topic of session IV–4. In this session we examine the decision of our lives, and consider how our faith is a style of life expressed in our day-by-day decisions. The heart of this session is a chart that you will want to be sure to have duplicated immediately if you have not already done so.

The final session of the course is entitled "The Spirit in Our Decisions." It recognizes that for Christians maturity is a dynamic quality of life that relates to a vitality of the Spirit of Christ. It affirms that the Christian faith will not alleviate our tensions, but will hold them in meaningful balance. It raises some searching questions about the decisions that need to be made in churches that are pussy-footing instead of responding boldly to the prompting of the Spirit.

Can I Love as Christ Does?

*What is Christianity? Suppose we asked
the Gallup Poll to sample the opinions of all the Americans
who attend Protestant church services on any one Sunday.
A composite summary probably would look something like this:
Beneath all the jargon of creed and doctrine,
beneath all the pomp of ceremony and ritual,
the secret power of Christianity always has been the appeal
of the ideals Jesus taught and the inspiration
of his wonderful life. . . . A true Christian is a person
who practices what Jesus preached.
To put it in a single sentence,
American Protestants tend to define Christian faith
as a "way of life" based on the moral ideals Jesus taught
and the good life Jesus lived.*

*Certainly Jesus Christ is the center
of Christian faith, and certainly Jesus as teacher
and example is indispensable to Christians. Yet this is not
all that the Bible and Christian tradition tell us
about Jesus, and it is not even the most important part
of the Christian gospel. Primary concentration on Jesus'
way of life has encouraged modern Protestants to fall into
a state of abysmal ignorance concerning the total, over–all
message of the Bible and Christian tradition.*[1]

Purpose of This Session

To get into the concluding unit on responding to the challenge in our Christian heritage; to do this by focusing on the question of what we should do in response to God's kind of love. This session is based on pages 96–105 of the resource book. It includes the study of Matthew 5:43–48 and John 13:34–35.

Background for the Leader

In unit III we have dealt at considerable length with the centrality of love in the Christian heritage. We have stressed the fact that Christian love is a special kind of love, characteristic of God, and manifest in human form in Christ. Though we have sometimes implied that such love is commanded of us, this has not been the dominant theme. For the most part we have been dealing with love as the nature of God.

Now we change the focus as we move into a unit in which we consider our response to the challenge in the Christian heritage. In this first session of unit IV the spotlight is on the kind of love God expects of us. Can I love as Christ does? is the question to which we adddress ourselves.

The answer seems to be that we can love God, our neighbors, and ourselves with this kind of love—but imperfectly. Since the command of God is that we love perfectly (see Matthew 5:43–48), our efforts at doing so forever remain an intention rather than an achievement. It must be this way if God is to remain God. If we ever achieved perfection, we would be equal to God. (See Matthew 19:17. Why did Jesus not want to be called good? What did he mean by saying, "One there is who is good"?)

It would be helpful if you would return to the study of the "Thought for the Leader" that heads session III–7 on page 96 of this coursebook. Also consider what is implied by the "Thought for the Leader" at the beginning of this session. This quotation calls attention to the real issue. Any consideration that leads to authentic Christian experience centers not in the examination of our goodness but in joy because of the good news of the kind of God we have. You will have a challenging but mountaintop experience in this session if you are able to help your group realize these things. The central goodness of the Christian religion resides in God. The opposite of sin is not goodness but faith.

Getting Started

You might center your opening discussion on two questions:

1. Can we love as Christ does? Perfectly?
2. What is the one main purpose of life?

These are questions with far-reaching implications. If you use them you will need to allow sufficient time for discussion. You might divide into small groups, with some considering the first question and others thinking about the second question.

Resource material for the first question is contained in pages 102–105 of the resource book. For question two, see pages 98–102 of the resource book. Also, the Westminster Confession affirms that man's purpose in life is "to glorify God, and to enjoy him for ever." What are some everyday implications of that statement of purpose?

Getting into Things

By this time you will probably be very much in the thick of things. In your group discussion, introduce the study of Matthew 5:43–48 and John 13:34–35. What do these passages mean? What does the group think is the import of pages 102–105 of the resource book? Can we love as Christ does? If not (as these resources claim), why should we keep trying to perfect God's kind of love?

Concluding and Looking Ahead

As a summary statement you might consider the essence of what is written in the preceding section, "Background for the Leader." You might also read to the group the "Thought for the Leader," followed by appropriate remarks about what is involved in an authentic Christian experience. In essence you will be saying that our purpose in life is not goodness. This is a by-product of glorifying God and enjoying him forever. Our purpose in life is intimately involved with God. We can, in joy, respond to God's grace with growth in grace—constantly striving after perfection!

Explain to your group that the next session will actually be a continuation of this one. It will concern the process of growing in grace. Ask that they prepare by studying pages 103–117 of the resource book.

Possibilities for Worship

Band 3 of *Hymns for Worship—Adults* (5 minutes)

Growing in Grace: the Process of Gratitude

Since then we are redeemed from our misery by grace through Christ, without any merit of ours, why must we do good works?

Because Christ, having redeemed us by his blood, renews us also by his Holy Spirit after his own image, that with our whole life we may show ourselves thankful to God for his blessing, and that He may be glorified through us; then also that we ourselves may be assured of our faith by the fruits thereof, and by our godly walk may win others also to Christ.[1]

Background for the Leader

One of the difficult questions of the Christian faith is: If God loves us without concern for merit, why should we try to live righteous lives? This session deals with this question, and asserts that the deepest motive for righteous living is gratitude to God.

As you discuss such matters the "Thought for the Leader" at the beginning of this session will be of considerable assistance. It consists of a question and answer from one of the catechisms.

In addition, you will find much resource material for this session in the following passage from a book on Christian ethics. It is our suggestion that you use these paragraphs both for your own study and as resource material for your group discussion.

We see here that, while our good works do not save us or earn us standing with God, they do figure in the picture at two points. We can never do more than God requires and we frequently do less; hence it can never be on our merits but by God's free gift—grace—that we are saved. But works are not as unimportant as some distortions of Christianity have assumed: good works are required by the law and God's measure of them is the judgment which makes us feel our need of redemption. Then our response to this free gift is a renewed striving to do good works—works which again we judge—and the cycle begins all over again. And though works are not the means of salvation they are signs by which we may know the reality of our repentance and justification. Truly, "By their fruits you shall know them," as our Lord said; and, contrary to what Luther thought, there is no real conflict between the Epistle of James, with its emphasis on works, and the teaching of St. Paul, with its emphasis on grace and faith. Faith without works *is* dead. If the promotion of goodness, or at least the delimitation of evil, does not come out of a supposed experience of justification, one can well doubt the reality of the whole experience or of one of its component parts—the repentance, the trust in God's forgiveness, or the firm purpose of amendment. St. Paul also exhorts us to do good works in every field of life. He is more precise about the relationship of these works to the full experience of the Christian life. His is a *therefore* ethic: since Christ has saved us, let us therefore behave in such a fashion. If we have really transferred our allegiance from false gods to the true God, inevitably we will do the works of the true God. Then we will have experienced the fullness of the process defined by St. Paul: "Justification by grace through faith unto good works." [2]

Purpose of This Session

To continue the exploration of what is involved in responding to the challenge in our Christian heritage; to recognize that our role is to respond to God's grace by ourselves growing in grace; to realize that growth in grace is a process of gratitude. This session is based on pages 103–117 of the resource book, *The Decision Maker*.

Getting Started

As persons arrive, engage them in total group discussion or in buzz groups on the question: In the Christian life of responding to the challenge in God's grace, is it more important to be good, or to be thankful? We would suggest that you pursue this discussion without benefit of resource material. When you have an idea of the opinions of the group, you might suggest that they find out what the resource book says on this subject. Refer them to pages 103–105 of *The Decision Maker*. You might also share with them the "Thought for the Leader" on page 106. As you can see by the pages in the resource book, we contend that thankfulness is more important than goodness, because it is the root of goodness.

Getting into Things

The above discussion will probably consume a goodly amount of time. When you think the appropriate moment has arrived, suggest that the group move into the next phase of the session. This would involve looking at the "Thought for the Leader," if you have not already done so, and also at Ephesians 2:1–10 and Matthew 18:23–35. With these biblical passages, the "Thought for the Leader," and pages 103–105 of *The Decision Maker* as resource material, you should have an interesting and provocative discussion.

If you have access to a copy of the Heidelberg Catechism you might call attention to its third section, entitled "Of Thankfulness" (*Von der Dankbarkeit*), and explain its view that thankfulness, thought of as the glad and free recognition of our infinite indebtedness to God, is the true motive of Christian living.

It would be well for you to budget considerable time for discussion of the suggested Bible references dealing with the question posed by this session. In Ephesians 2 pay particular attention to verses 8, 9, and 10. Note how they say that salvation is a gift of God, "not because of works, lest any man should boast," yet they claim that "we are his workmanship, created in Christ Jesus for good works, which God prepared beforehand, that we should walk in them." In this regard, see the "Thought for the Leader" on page 106 of this coursebook.

In your study of Matthew 18 pay special attention to verses 32 and 33. We are forever indebted to God for his grace and mercy. Our lot is to be grateful for it, and to live gratefully.

Another idea, related to these but in need of special attention, is that this expression of gratitude that motivates the Christian life is a continuous and continual *process*. In this regard you may want to have someone read aloud pages 104–105 of the resource book. What are some of the implications of this for our lives?

Concluding and Looking Ahead

Have a member of the group summarize the developments of this session. You will want to talk with him in advance about this assignment, so that he will be ready for his role when the proper time for it arrives in your session. A way of focusing your summary might be to address yourselves to deciding how you would now answer the question, Are you saved?

Ask members of the group to study chapter 10 of the resource book in preparation for the next session.

Possibilities for Worship

Ephesians 2:1–10
Hymn: "Take Thou Our Minds, Dear Lord"
Prayer
or
Band 3, *Hymns for Worship—Adult* (5 minutes)

Freedom in Captivity

Make me a captive, Lord,
And then I shall be free;
Force me to render up my sword,
And I shall conqueror be.
I sink in life's alarms,
When by myself I stand;
Imprison me within Thine arms,
And strong shall be my hand.

My heart is weak and poor
Until it master find;
It has no spring of action sure—
It varies with the wind;
It cannot freely move
Till Thou has wrought its chain;
Enslave it with Thy matchless love,
And deathless it shall reign.

* * *

My will is not my own
Till Thou hast made it Thine;
If it would reach a monarch's throne,
It must its crown resign:
It only stands unbent
Amid the clashing strife,
When on Thy bosom it has leant,
And found in Thee its life.[1]

Purpose of This Session

To explore the meaning of Christian discipleship; to see that our extremely high destiny is most nearly realized when we are captive to the will of God; to recognize and marvel at the great Christian paradox of freedom in captivity. This session is based on part of chapter 10 of the resource book, pages 106–116.

Getting Started

If you want a kind of pre-session activity for this session, you might ask the members of your group to meditate on the words of the theme hymn for the course, "Make Me a Captive, Lord." There is much in this hymn to commend it for meditation!

Getting into Things

There are some extremely important passages of scripture dealing with this subject which we suggest that your group study during this session. Two of these are Galatians 5:13–26 and Romans 6:15–23. Romans 6:22 is especially significant, and we suggest that you "major" on this verse.

If time permits you might have the entire group (or small study groups) explore first Galatians 5:13–26 and then Romans 6:15–23. If time is short you might have half the group consider one passage while the rest study the other.

The thing to look for in this study is: What does the author of this course mean when he talks about freedom in captivity? Is he correct in what he says in the resource book chapter on this subject? (chapter 10)

After considerable discussion you might ask everyone in the group to focus on Romans 6:22. Ask them to write out in their own words what this verse really says. Call for volunteers to read what they have written, and use these reports as a basis for discussion.

Concluding and Looking Ahead

How does the group feel about the resource book's statements on freedom in captivity? Does the concept mean anything important to the Christian life? How does it relate to our decisions? our everyday lives? What does it say about the role of the Bible in our lives? (See page 121 of the resource book.) about the role of prayer? (See page 121.) about worship? (See page 122.)

Lead the group now in looking ahead to the next session. Point out that pages 113-122 of *The Decision Maker* are its basis, and ask them to study these pages in preparation for the next session.

Possibilities for Worship

Scripture: Romans 6:15–23
Hymn: "Make Me a Captive, Lord"
Prayer: The words of the hymn
or
Band 5, *Hymns for Worship—Adults* (2½ minutes)

Responsible Decision-Making

*God has given man a unique capacity
to know and to respond to him. He created him in his
own image for eternal life. God offered man the knowledge of
good and evil. But such knowledge can be received only by
the taking. It comes through the making of choices
and the discovering of consequences. By the freedom to
make real choices involving good and evil, God let
man become real. He did not want puppets.*[1]

Purpose of This Session

To explore the process of making decisions; to differentiate between *the* decision and daily decisions; to see how our faith is expressed through our decisions and their consequences. This session is based on pages 113–122 of the resource book.

Getting Started

As persons arrive, ask them to discuss in small groups the question: What goes into the making of a decision? After a few minutes begin the all-group session, and give a brief introduction to the session, making sure your purpose is understood.

Getting into Things

The heart of this session is the form for listing the factors that influence our decisions (see page 115). Since this is the cornerstone of this unit, be sure to have plenty of copies available for this session.

Introduce these forms carefully and completely. Remind the members of the group that the forms will not be easy to complete, but that they will require considerable thought if the results are to have any significance. The main point is to discover what factors really are determining the direction of our lives.

One question that may arise is whether this form calls for listing factors in past experience that continue to influence our decisions today, or whether it asks only for current influences. You might suggest that they include all influences, past or present: such factors as wife or husband, money, law, Bible, job, friends, pleasure, church, God, reputation, health, and so on.

When the group has had enough time for filling out these forms, ask several members to name two or three factors that influence their decisions, and you might list these on the chalkboard. Be especially concerned to note any reference to God (church, Jesus Christ, and so forth) as an influence in our decisions, and how frequently God is an influence: often, fairly often, or not very often. How many persons in the group listed God as an influence? Ask the group, What does this indicate about our style of living?

Now discuss the following questions: What is the difference between *the* decision of our lives, and our daily decisions? What is conversion? Is it a necessary part of the Christian life? For those of us who have not known one dramatic moment of decision, is there no element of *the* decision in our lives? If there is, how would you explain it? What is the relationship of *the* decision to the everyday decisions of our lives? What is the role of our daily decisions in the expression of faith? What is faith? What about the statements on pages 113–120 of the resource book?

Concluding

You might use Joshua 24:14–15 and Acts 21:13–14 as your conclusion. The Christian life is one of responsible decision making! As such, God is the primary influence in our decisions! Or is he?

Possibilities for Worship

Scripture: Joshua 24:14–15 and Acts 21:13–14
Hymn: Make Me a Captive, Lord"
Prayer
or
Band 5, *Hymns for Worship—Adults* (2¼ minutes)

FACTORS INFLUENCING MY DECISIONS	Place of Decision				Frequency of Influence		
	Church	Home	Work	Other	Often	Fairly Often	Not Very Often
1.							
2.							
3.							
4.							
5.							
6.							
7.							

The Spirit in Our Decisions

The very hollowness of man's center, however, God meant for himself. Only when God is truly the center of man's life, can man escape the insecurity that tempts him to curve in on himself, or to lean on others as means to his own safety, and to be faithless toward God.

When God the eternal Spirit fills man's central hollowness, on the contrary, man accepts himself, finds true community, and lives in peace and power with God. Thus man's essential goodness is his potential goodness. His sin is holding God off. The more he knows God, the greater the sin.

If freedom is to be real and God's good freely chosen, man needs this experience. He needs to be alienated from God. To say so is not to make light of sin, but to honor God's way of working. The more and the sooner God is accepted as central, however, the better. It is God's will and man's destiny that God become thus central. . . . Man is made for the Love God is. . . .[1]

Purpose of This Session

To explore the Christian understanding of maturity, security, and success. To recognize the presence of the Holy Spirit in making daily decisions; to think about continuing our consciousness of the Spirit in all our decisions.

Getting Started

We would suggest dividing your group into three small groups (or, if the group is very large, into several groups of four to seven persons each). As persons arrive for the session, give some the statement, "Describe Maturity"; others, "Describe Security"; and still others, "Describe Success." Have pencils and paper available.

Another way to begin would be to ask all members of the group to describe the Holy Spirit.

Still another way to get started would be to have persons or groups study Acts 2:1–21, and discuss these questions:

1. What was the role of the Spirit in the lives of these people?
2. What is the role of the Spirit today?
3. What is the role of the Spirit in our everyday decisions?

Getting into Things

The purpose of this session is to conclude the course with some understanding of what is involved in the Christian view of man's nature and purpose. Nowhere does the gospel allow us to resolve our tensions, or to formulate simple and final answers. But it does help to hold our tensions and frustrations in balance.

You will find a discussion of the nature of Christian maturity, success, and security in the final chapter of the resource book. Such maturity, success and security calls us to be Christian decision makers, free in captivity to God, or responsibly free. The Spirit, God alive today, God contemporary, is the primary factor in the endless process of gratitude in which we are engaged.

The challenge is to achieve, to accept, and to continue the consciousness of the Spirit in our everyday, work-a-world decisions.

Really Getting into Things

As the resource book affirms on page 84, the Christian life is never lived in isolation, but always in community. The covenant is made with the community of God's chosen people, the church—not with individuals. As you conclude this course, we suggest that you really get into some of the issues involved in making decisions responsibly in freedom. Our suggestion is that you do this by making use of the pamphlet *Stop Pussyfooting Through a Revolution*. We hope that you will be able to obtain at least a few copies of this booklet, if you do not already have some. The booklet is included in the 1963–64 *Program Opportunities for Adults*, published by the Council for Lay Life and Work.

We think that the following paragraphs would be especially helpful in starting discussion on some of the crucial decisions your church will need to make. What is a mature response to the prompting of the Holy Spirit, in light of these paragraphs? What do they suggest regarding ways in which we might follow up this course?

The church has been accused of acting like a modern Rip Van Winkle. It has been sleeping through the urban revolution now pervading the world.

But this is not a true diagnosis of the situation. For the church is not simply *sleeping* through a revolution; it is too often *pussyfooting* through it. The church has not been helping people to understand the issues and problems of that revolution, nor to solve them so that these people can live well in an urban world. . . .

God has given us full and unique weaponry for becoming involved with him in ministering to human need. The modern form of putting on the whole armor of God demands:

—A complete view of the world and of the life in this world which enables us to take the Bible seriously and to wrestle with the relevance of the Scriptures for the contemporary situation.

—A community so open to God that it concerns itself with proclaiming Christ and with witnessing for him to all sorts and conditions of men. . . .

—A sharp insight into the manner in which God is presently at work in the phenomenon of urbanization, both in the forms that appear to be constructive and in those that appear to be destructive.

—An acute sensitivity to the needs of city people, including the all-important sensitivity of becoming partners with these people so that both church and people realize that God judges them equally and that neither can be lifted to a new and more complete life without the other.

—A sanctified imagination—and yet a discipline—which faces facts and thereby raises up new congregations which will initiate change, innovation, development, and invention.

In short, the present behavior pattern of our Christian churches, which relies on pussyfooting, must be reversed. We must stop escaping involvement. We must stop running away. We must no longer simply merge with the people who happen to be our cup of tea. We must escape from our ivory towers. We must take *new* steps. We must walk in the marketplace among the realities of existence, where men, in the modern vernacular, have not only been branded as the meanest of bastards but actually go out of their way to live up to the epithet. And we must walk there with dignity and courage, compassion and humility.

This means that we ought to get to the marketplace as quickly as possible, even if it means going native in the matters of faith and morals. It may, in fact, do us good to upset a few moral taboos. Some of us may even have to be sensitive to God's demands by refusing to be churchmen! [2]

Concluding

Try to save some time for discussing questions and comments about the entire course. It would be ideal if you could save the final fifteen minutes for having members of the group fill out evaluation forms (see page 20) giving their reactions to the entire course.

Before this, however, call attention again to the two teaching pictures "The Children of Israel Worshiping the Golden Calf" by Poussin, and "The Last Supper" by Fra Angelico. Ask the questions: Do *we* ever worship golden calves? What is the role of the Lord's Supper in the Christian life? Summarize the thinking of the group, and then refer to our need of the new covenant by which Christ not only redeems us, but also empowers us to fulfill our essential nature, our high status under God, enabling us to make more and more decisions freely in captivity to God.

A good question to leave with members of the group, unanswered, might be: What, then, is Christian decision-making?

Possibilities for Worship

Band 5, *Hymns for Worship—Adults* (2½ minutes)

Steering or Evaluation Committee

Be sure to arrange for a small group of persons to join you in evaluation of the course and planning for whatever follow-up may seem appropriate.

ACKNOWLEDGMENTS

UNIT I

Session 1

1. From *Know Your Faith* by Nels F. S. Ferré. Copyright by Nels F. S. Ferré, 1959. (Pp. 58–60, 62.) Reprinted by permission of Harper & Row, Publishers, Incorporated, New York.

Session 2

1. Nels F. S. Ferré, *Know Your Faith.* (Pp. 62–63.)

Session 3

1. David E. Roberts, *The Grandeur and Misery of Man.* Copyright 1955 by Oxford University Press, Inc. New York. (Pp.143–144.)

UNIT II

Session 1

1. Gerald Kennedy in *The Interpreter's Bible,* Volume 6. Copyright © 1956 by Pierce and Washabaugh. (Pp. 394–397.) Used by permission of Abingdon Press, Nashville.

Session 2

1. A. Roy Eckardt, *The Surge of Piety in America.* Copyright © 1958 by National Board of Young Men's Christian Association. (P. 49.) Used by permission of Association Press, New York.

Session 3

1. Charles T. Sardeson, *Rediscovering the Words of Faith.* Copyright 1956 by Pierce and Washabaugh. (P. 88.) Used by permission of Abingdon Press, Nashville.

Session 4

1. Charles T. Sardeson, *Rediscovering the Words of Faith.* (Pp. 89–90.)

Session 5

1. Nels F. S. Ferré, *Know Your Faith.* (Pp. 71–72.)
2. Cuthbert A. Simpson in *The Interpreter's Bible,* Volume 1. Copyright 1952 by Pierce and Smith. (P. 485.) Used by permission of Abingdon Press, Nashville.
3. Cuthbert A. Simpson in *The Interpreter's Bible,* Volume 1. (P. 483.)
4. Francis W. Beare in *The Interpreter's Bible,* Volume 11. Copyright 1955 by Pierce and Washabaugh. (P. 164.) Used by permission of Abingdon Press, Nashville.

Session 6

1. Oliver Powell, *Seed and Soil,* copyright 1963 by the United Church Press, Boston and Philadelphia. (P. 29.)

UNIT III

Session 1

1. Charles T. Sardeson, *Rediscovering the Words of Faith.* (P. 36.)

Session 2

1. Nels F. S. Ferré, *Know Your Faith.* (P. 75.)

Session 3

1. From "The Faith of Israel" by G. Ernest Wright. *The Interpreter's Bible,* Volume 1. (P. 382.)

Session 4

1. From "Insights into Christian Love" by Clement of Rome. The translation is that of Alexander Roberts and James Donaldson in *The Ante-Nicene Fathers* (New York, 1885).
2. Adapted from *We Believe,* 1958 Programs for Leaders of Adult Groups, by Robert V. Moss, Jr. (Pp. 61–64.) Used by permission of the author.

Session 5

1. Reuel L. Howe, *Herein Is Love.* Copyright 1961 by The Judson Press, Valley Forge, Pa. (Pp. 44–45.) Used by permission.

Session 6

1. Dietrich Bonhoeffer, *The Cost of Discipleship.* Copyright 1959. (Pp. 36–37.) Used by permission of The Macmillan Company, New York, and the Student Christian Movement Press Ltd., London.
2. John McIntyre, *On the Love of God.* Copyright © 1962 by John McIntyre. (Pp. 35–36.) Used by permission of Harper & Row, Publishers, Incorporated, New York, and Wm. Collins Sons & Co., Ltd., London.

Session 7

1. Reprinted with the permission of Charles Scribner's Sons, New York, and James Nisbet & Co., Ltd., London, from *The Nature and Destiny of Man,* Vol. II, pp. 125–6, by Reinhold Niebuhr. Copyright 1943 Charles Scribner's Sons.

UNIT IV

Session 1

1. From *Modern Rivals to Christian Faith* by Cornelius Loew. Copyright 1956, W. L. Jenkins. (Pp. 71–72.) The Westminster Press, Philadelphia. Used by permission.

Session 2

1. *Heidelberg Catechism,* Question 86 and its Answer.
2. From *Doing the Truth* by James A. Pike. Copyright © 1955 by James A. Pike. (Pp. 93–94.) Reprinted by permission of Doubleday & Company, Inc., New York, and Victor Gollancz, Ltd., London.

Session 3

1. George Matheson, "Make Me a Captive, Lord."

Session 4

1. Nels F. S. Ferré, *Know Your Faith.* (Pp. 62–63.)

Session 5

1. Nels F. S. Ferré, *Know Your Faith.* (Pp. 64–65.)
2. J. Archie Hargraves, *Stop Pussyfooting Through a Revolution,* Stewardship Council of the United Church of Christ, 1963. (Pp. 2–3.)

BIBLICAL REFERENCES